Set for Act One (and Act Three) of the Dallas Theater Center production of "Lu Ann Hampton Laverty Oberlander." Designed by Mary Sue Jones.

LU ANN HAMPTON LAVERTY OBERLANDER

A PLAY IN THREE ACTS
BY PRESTON JONES

(One of the three plays comprising
A TEXAS TRILOGY)

DRAMATISTS
PLAY SERVICE
INC.

To my beloved wife, Mary Sue

SOUND EFFECTS RECORD

The following sound effects record, which may be used in connection with production of this play, can be obtained from Thomas J. Valentino, Inc., 151 West 46th Street, New York, NY 10036.

No. 5025 — Telephone ring

LU ANN HAMPTON LAVERTY OBERLANDER was first presented in New York City by Robert Whitehead and Roger L. Stevens (as one of three full-length plays in repertory collectively entitled A TEXAS TRILOGY*) at the Broadhurst Theatre on September 21, 1976. It was directed by Alan Schneider; the scenery and lighting were by Ben Edwards; and the costumes were by Jane Greenwood. The assistant director was Joan Thorne. The cast, in order of appearance, was as follows:

CLAUDINE HAMPTON .... Avril Gentles
LU ANN HAMPTON .... Diane Ladd
BILLY BOB WORTMAN .... James Staley
SKIP HAMPTON .... Graham Beckel
DALE LAVERTY .... Everett McGill
RUFE PHELPS .... Walter Flanagan
OLIN POTTS .... Thomas Toner
RED GROVER .... Patrick Hines
CORKY OBERLANDER .... Baxter Harris
MILO CRAWFORD .... Josh Mostel
CHARMAINE .... Kristin Griffith

SCENES: Bradleyville, Texas
ACT I: The Hampton Home, 1953
ACT II: Red Grover's Bar, 1963
ACT III: The Hampton Home, 1973

(When A TEXAS TRILOGY was first performed at the Kennedy Center, in Washington, D.C., the part of Claudine Hampton was played by Kate Wilkinson and Charmaine by Janet Grey.)

*Consisting of THE LAST MEETING OF THE KNIGHTS OF THE WHITE MAGNOLIA, LU ANN HAMPTON LAVERTY OBERLANDER and THE OLDEST LIVING GRADUATE.

Background information for A TEXAS TRILOGY:

Author's Note

An extraordinary energy in the theater is the energy of the playwright. It tells us things. It gives us life as no other element of theater can. It is relentless and often difficult. So, pay attention.

PAUL BAKER

For a playwright, there can be no greater thrill than to see his plays first come to life on the stage. Therefore, I look back with special fondness to the fall of 1973 when the Dallas Theater Center began work on *A Texas Trilogy*. As a member of the Theater Center since 1962, I had come to appreciate the hard work and lively creativity that surround each production. This became especially clear to me when the trilogy plays were produced under the direction of Paul Baker.

The Dallas Theater Center has a tradition of producing original plays because Paul Baker is committed to supporting the playwright on both artistic and economic levels. My plays, and those of other writers, have grown out of this nourishing atmosphere, one which encourages each new play to find its way.

Rehearsals for *A Texas Trilogy* were creative enterprises involving everyone. Lines were added and cut, plots were strengthened. Schemes were devised to help actors understand the social and environmental aspects of Bradleyville. In order to deepen their characterizations, actors were asked to construct collages designed to capture, in textural forms, the basic elements of each character's past life. These and other techniques used throughout rehearsals of the three plays were valuable and stimulating to all of us—director, designer, actors, and playwright alike.

For this enriching experience I am grateful to Paul Baker, Eugene McKinney, Randy Moore, Ken Latimer, Sallie Laurie, Mona Pursley, Robyn Flatt, James Crump, John Henson, Synthia Rodgers, John Logan, Tim Green, William Landrey, Allen Hibbard, Tommy Kendrick, Ted

6

Mitchell, Sam Nance, Keith Dixon, Chris McCarty, Charles Beachley, Roger Richards, Matt Tracy, and Rebecca Ramsey. I wish to acknowledge my appreciation to these fine artists and true first citizens of Bradleyville.

The Last Meeting of the Knights of the White Magnolia was first performed at the Down Center Stage of the Dallas Theater Center on December 4, 1973. Two months later, on February 5, 1974, *Lu Ann Hampton Laverty Oberlander* premiered at the same theater. Then, beginning on November 19, 1974, with *The Oldest Living Graduate*, all three plays were produced in repertory on the Dallas Theater Center's main stage, the Kalita Humphreys Theater. Performances were under the direction of Paul Baker and cast from the resident company and graduate apprentices at the Dallas Theater Center.

The Last Meeting of the Knights of the White Magnolia was chosen by the American Playwrights Theatre as its 1975-76 offering, and the play has been produced by numerous regional, university, civic, and professional theaters across the country.

Starting on April 29, 1976, the John F. Kennedy Center for the Performing Arts presented *A Texas Trilogy* in repertory at its Eisenhower Theater in Washington, D.C. The plays, which ran for a ten-week season under the direction of Alan Schneider, were produced by Robert Whitehead and Roger L. Stevens. On August 5, 1976, the trilogy was brought back to the Kennedy Center for a five-week run prior to its New York opening.

The Place

Bradleyville, Texas—population 6,000—a small, dead West Texas town in the middle of a big, dead West Texas prairie between Abilene and San Angelo. The new highway has bypassed it and now the world is trying to.

The People

THE HAMPTON FAMILY

CLAUDINE HAMPTON attended high school in Bradleyville and, through a program at the hospital, became a practical nurse. She married Lloyd Hampton. Lloyd worked for the refinery until his death in 1945. Claudine has two children, Skip and Lu Ann. Both of them are grown now but still remain a great source of worry to her. Mrs. Hampton is well known in town for her ability and honesty.

SKIP HAMPTON was born and raised in Bradleyville, graduating from high school and serving in the army during the Korean War. In his entire life Skip has never been able to distinguish himself in any type of endeavor. If you look in his *Senior Year Annual* from Bradleyville High, you'll find under his picture the name Skip Hampton and nothing else. During Korea, Skip drove a supply truck—never getting closer to the front than sixty miles; however, with the passage of time and especially after many drinks, his war record gets bloodier and bloodier. After the war Skip tried several get-rich-quick schemes that always melted in his hands. Then he discovered the bottle. Skip is unmarried and lives with his mother and sister. He pumps gas for a living and has finally been able to distinguish himself in the eyes of all Bradleyville. He is the town drunk.

LU ANN HAMPTON was born at the Bradleyville Memorial Hospital in 1936. She suffered through the usual amount of bites, cuts, scratches, bruises, and minor childhood ailments, but never knew real heartbreak until her father died in 1945. Another blow came when her best friend moved to California in 1947.

Always a popular girl in school, Lu Ann held several offices. She was co-editor of the grade school *Messenger*, and member of the Pepettes drill team. In high school, she was four times elected to the student senate as the representative of Miss Scott's home room and was, in her sophomore year, Future Farmers of America Sweetheart and class yearbook reporter.

She could have held many more offices, but the demanding chores of being Head Cheerleader for the past two years have forced her to curtail many activities. Lu Ann lives with her mother and brother at 301 Grand Street and goes steady with Billy Bob Wortman. After graduation from high school, she plans "to have lots and lots of fun."

CHARMAINE is Lu Ann's daughter by Dale Laverty. After Corky Oberlander was killed, Lu Ann moved back into her mother's house and Charmaine was brought up there. She is spoiled and pampered by her mother, her grandmother, and her uncle.

Charmaine became the child of an unsettled household and unsettled times. As the years passed, she grew ashamed of her mother, contemptuous of her uncle, and utterly unseeing of her invalid grandmother. Her school grades are bad, her outlook bleak, her lifestyle slovenly and wasteful, but maybe all these negatives equip her better than her mother for today's times.

BILLY BOB WORTMAN lives with his mother, father, and three younger sisters in a small house on Austin Street. Always interested in agriculture, Billy Bob has been a member of Future Farmers of America since 1947, and his entries have won many prizes at the Mumford County Fair. Now, in his senior year in high school, Billy Bob is an Eagle Scout, a Y.M.C.A. summer camp counselor, and a starting forward on the varsity basketball team.

Next to his father, Billy Bob considers Reverend Stone of the First Christian Church one of the finest men that ever lived. Billy Bob started going steady with Lu Ann Hampton at the beginning of his senior year, right after she had broken up with Floyd Tatum and he had broken up with Eveline Blair. (Ruthie Lee Lawell got them together at a sock-hop.)

Billy Bob isn't too sure what his plans are after graduation, but you can bet whatever it is, it will have something to do with basketball and the Lord.

DALE LAVERTY was born and raised in San Angelo, Texas. Always a big kid, Dale was known as Tubby Rump until he made first-string tackle on the football team and became known as the Hulk.

Dale's father was a truck driver and trucks became the passion of Dale's life. He dreamed of them. He saw himself in the cab rolling along in his own rig, booming across the Western plains, free and easy with the girls at the brightly lit truck stops. He would dream of swinging out of the cab and eating hugely on ham and eggs, great bowls of chili, fat-dripping cheeseburgers, and chicken-fried steak swimming and bubbling in heavy gravy.

Dale would like to be the hood ornament of a Mack truck, solid, heavy, tough, staring down the road in open-eyed defiance.

After the Korean War, in which he served as a truck driver, Dale came home with great goals in mind. He wished for a wife, a trailer house, a new Chevy, and a job driving semis. Man's needs are simple and his wants are few, but his lusts are strong and of great variety.

CORKY OBERLANDER was born into a German Lutheran family on a cotton farm outside Roscoe, Texas. He graduated from high school and served a hitch in the army engineers. Afterward, he returned home and used his army-learned surveying skills to get a job with the Highway Department in Abilene.

In 1959, Corky married Peggy Sue Roberts from Sweetwater. The marriage lasted only a few short months before she ran off with a core drill operator. (Peggy Sue always was about half-wild.) After the divorce, Corky spent a weekend getting drunk and laid in Juarez, Mexico. Then he stoically went back to work.

Corky likes to fish, hunt, play softball, and drink a few beers. He was having a few beers when he found himself at Red Grover's bar in Bradleyville and met a young lady named Lu Ann Hampton Laverty.

TOWN FOLK

L. D. ALEXANDER grew up in Bradleyville and married his high-school sweetheart. After his return from World War II, L.D. went to work for A.B.C. Supermarkets, Inc. He soon rose to the rank of manager, a modest but respectable position in Bradleyville's middle-class society. L.D. has two children, a boy and a girl. L.D. believes in white supremacy. L.D. is the guy with the green apron and the tag that says MGR. He is usually standing around the checkout stand.

RAMSEY-EYES BLANKENSHIP has lived in Bradleyville since he was ten years old and has known the secondhand existence of a West Texas black. In his own world, he is simply known as Granddaddy; in the white world he is Ramsey-Eyes. His full name, Ramsey Washington Blankenship has been used twice—once when he was baptized and once when he was married. It will not be used again until his funeral. Since the death of his wife, Ramsey-Eyes has lived by himself in a small, sagging, three-room house. Most of his children have moved to bigger cities and his grandchildren upset him with their mutterings about social change. As long as Ramsey-Eyes can earn his keep and go fishing every weekend, then he is content. He moves through his old age like a shuffling shadow.

MILO CRAWFORD was born and raised in Bradleyville. He was five years old when his father died, and Milo, an only child, came under his mother's grip. After graduating from high school, Milo was spared the draft when his mother claimed he was her sole support. For many years now Milo has worked at the Bradleyville Grain and Feed Store. Milo has contemplated marriage now and again, but the thought of leaving Mama is too painful for him to get seriously involved with a bride-to-be. Milo has made two great decisions in his life without consulting Mama: one, to take up cigarette smoking, and the other, to join the Knights of the White Magnolia, both decisions being mild forms of rebellion. To counteract these moves, Mama hides the ashtrays and tries to think up little errands for him to run on meeting nights.

RED GROVER is originally from Meridian, Mississippi. Red came to Bradleyville following its brief oil boom right after World War II, a conflict he served in totally without distinction. When the "homecoming G.I.'s" defeated the Baptists in the local "wet, dry election," Red took his savings and put up Red's Place, a bar and package liquor store. When the boom had run itself out and the wells were capped, Red found himself shunned by most of the townspeople and, like most bar owners, developed a deep disgust for his clients. Never taking a wife, Red rides out his sexual desires on skinny-legged barmaids and drunken divorcees and grows more and more bitter as the days and nights drag on.

RUFE PHELPS as a young man worked in various oil fields around West Texas. However, after he married, he settled down to a more permanent position at the refinery.

OLIN POTTS grew up on a family farm and stayed there. He married late in life and lives out at his place with his wife and mother. Olin and Rufe are both childless and have kept up a competitive struggle that began in grade school. They went through their softball and rodeo stage and are now hard at each other at checkers, fishing, dove hunting, horseshoes, and dominoes. Their ages and occupations kept them out of World War II and they spent the war years running trotlines and betting on the outcome of battles.

MIKE TREMAINE has lived in Bradleyville all his life. He is married and has three children. Mike grows watermelon and cotton on a small farm outside of town. He also works as general handyman for Floyd Kinkaid and has done so for about a year.

THE KINKAID FAMILY

COLONEL J. C. KINKAID is old and confined to a wheelchair. He was born in 1887 on his father's ranch, and in his youth he enjoyed the soft life that a cattle and cotton empire could provide. In his later years the God of Fortune that looks down on and loves us all added a further bonanza to him in the form of oil wells. He attended high school at Mirabeau B. Lamar Military Academy and went on to Texas A&M, choosing a military career over ranch life. The Colonel served with General John Pershing in the Philippines, in Mexico, and finally in France during World War I. What started out to be a fulfilling military career in the Philippines ended in the trenches in France. "The Colonel returned from the great war to continue in his family's business interests in and around Bradleyville, Texas, and is interested in many civic organizations," or so his paragraph reads in the *Texas Who's Who*. Actually, the Colonel returned from France shattered in mind and body. Luckily for the family, an older brother kept the fortune together until the Colonel's son Floyd took up his father's half of the business and simply let the Colonel ramble on into his lost world of memories. Now in his dotage, the Colonel's string is starting to run out.

FLOYD KINKAID is a power in this small town and he knows it. Floyd's interests are many and his hobbies are expensive: registered quarter horses, a big flashy bass boat, charter membership in the country club. He was twice president of the Jaycees and is a leading figure in all civic organizations. Floyd and his older brother, Franklin, were both born in Bradleyville after the Colonel's return from World War I. They attended Bradleyville High and both graduated from college—Franklin from Texas A&M and Floyd from Texas Tech. When World War II broke out, Franklin went into the air force and Floyd joined the navy. Franklin was killed when his B-17 crashed in Florida, and Floyd wound up attached to a headquarters section in San Diego. After the war, Floyd married Maureen and returned to Bradleyville to take control of his father's business interests. Floyd and his Uncle Brewster Kinkaid have turned the

Kinkaid holdings into a sizable money-making venture. Now, with the business virtually running itself, Floyd is becoming bored and is casting about for other interests.

MAUREEN KINKAID was born in Bradleyville of a moderately well-to-do family. She graduated from Bradleyville High and went on to Texas Tech, majoring in secondary education. She and Floyd had dated all through high school and had planned to get married after graduating from college. However, the war changed all that. Floyd went into the navy and Maureen did her bit on the Bradleyville home front answering "V" mail and collecting tinfoil. When the war was over, she and Floyd married and set up housekeeping in town. In 1957 Floyd built the new house and they moved to their present location. They have no children. Floyd secretly blames her and she secretly blames him, but neither has bothered to find out anything for sure. Maureen wonders why she's so goddamned bored with everything.

THE SICKENGER FAMILY

MARTHA ANN SICKENGER is also a Bradleyville girl. Her family owns the grain and feed store. Martha Ann graduated from high school in 1953 and was considered at the time to be "a little bit on the wild side." After a disastrous one semester at Texas University, Martha Ann returned home and grabbed off Clarence Sickenger, much to the town's amusement, Clarence being thirty-four at the time. However, their two children, Howard and Charlotte Marie, came bouncing into being and everybody came around to admitting that it might be a pretty good match after all. Martha Ann seems to think so, and if Clarence just happens to be one of the richest men in town, well, "what the hell."

CLARENCE SICKENGER is also a lifelong Bradleyville citizen; like Floyd, he too comes from a wealthy family. He graduated from Texas University and spent World War II right in Bradleyville—exempt from the draft because of his value to the oil industry. In 1953, Clarence married Martha Ann Montgomery and they settled down to a life of small-town wealth. Although Clarence and Floyd have never been close friends, they started a conversation out at the country-club bar the other day that had the makings of a real partnership.

Characters

LU ANN HAMPTON

SKIP HAMPTON

CLAUDINE HAMPTON

BILLY BOB WORTMAN

DALE LAVERTY

RED GROVER

RUFE PHELPS

OLIN POTTS

CORKY OBERLANDER

MILO CRAWFORD

CHARMAINE

LU ANN HAMPTON
LAVERTY OBERLANDER

ACT I

The time is 1953. The act is set in the living room of Claudine and Lu Ann Hampton's home in Bradleyville. A small frame house in a small frame town. The room is modestly furnished in Sears-catalogue-type furniture—sofa, table, chairs, radio, etc. A door Upstage Left leads to the kitchen. Upstage Center door leads to bedrooms. Stage Right is a small front porch section with a functional screen door.

As the scene opens, Claudine slams through the kitchen door with bowl of tangerines, sets it on end table. She is a heavy-set woman in her early forties, her hair is grayish blond. She is dressed in house dress and apron—takes apron off and puts it on sofa back. Notes time and looks out porch door, then exits back into the kitchen. Lu Ann runs on and into living room. She is dressed in the blue-and-gold uniform of a Bradleyville cheerleader. She is well built and very blond. She is also very pretty. Small-town pretty, healthy pretty, clean pretty, Pepsodent and Ivory Soap pretty.

BILLY BOB. (*Offstage.*) Lu Ann! Lu Ann! Wait up, will ya! (*Following Lu Ann on. Billy Bob Wortman is tall and lanky. He wears a white shirt, Levi's, boots, and a letter sweater. His crew-cut hair has been dyed green.*)
LU ANN. Ma! I'm home!
CLAUDINE. (*Offstage.*) About time!
LU ANN. Well, ah thought ah would die! Ah jest thought ah would curl up and die right there on the gym floor. When the coach introduced the basketball team and you-all come out there with your hair all dyed green. Well, sir, mah eyes liked to jumped plumb outta mah head! Why, Mary Beth Johnson jest hollered. That's right, jest hollered right out loud.
BILLY BOB. It was Pete Honeycutt's idea.
LU ANN. Why, ever'one jest laughed and shouted and carried on so.

Eveline Blair came runnin' over to me shoutin', "Look at the basketball boys, look at the basketball boys!"

BILLY BOB. It was Pete Honeycutt's idea.

LU ANN. (*Gestures to porch—they go out.*) After the assembly we cheerleaders all got together and decided we'd do somethin' funny too.

BILLY BOB. Aw, like what?

LU ANN. Now wouldn't you like to know? Mr. Green-headed Billy Bob Wortman.

BILLY BOB. Aw, come on, Lu Ann, what are you-all fixin' to do?

LU ANN. Oh, ah don't know, somethin', somethin' real neat.

BILLY BOB. You cain't dye you-all's hair. Pete Honeycutt already thought that one up.

LU ANN. Eveline Blair thought up different shoes.

BILLY BOB. Different shoes?

LU ANN. You know, come to school wearin' one high-heel shoe and one saddle shoe. Somethin' *neato* like that.

BILLY BOB. Yeah.

LU ANN. Ah don't know, though, it might be kinda tricky doin' the Locomotive in a high-heel shoe.

BILLY BOB. Might be at that.

LU ANN. But it might be fun.

BILLY BOB. Shore.

LU ANN. (*Sitting on swing.*) Maybe we can wear them out to the senior picnic.

BILLY BOB. (*Joins her.*) Shore!

LU ANN. We're still goin' in your daddy's Hudson, ain't we?

BILLY BOB. Well, uh, naw, we gotta use the pickup.

LU ANN. The pickup!

BILLY BOB. Yeah, my dad wants the car to go over to Big Spring.

LU ANN. But it's the senior picnic! Mah God, ah don't want to go to mah one and only senior picnic in a danged-old pickup.

BILLY BOB. Well, goshalmighty, Lu Ann, ah cain't help it.

LU ANN. What the heck good is it for your dad to have a bran'-new, step-down Hudson Hornet if *we* never get to use the danged old thing.

BILLY BOB. Seems like ever'thin' ah do is wrong.

LU ANN. Boy, that's the truth.

BILLY BOB. Gawlee, Ruthie Lee Lawell and Pete Honeycutt are goin' in his pickup.

LU ANN. So what.

BILLY BOB. Well, nuthin', ah jest mean that it don't seem to bother Ruthie Lee none.

LU ANN. Heck no, it don't bother Ruthie Lee none. Mah Gawd, she

16

almost lives in Pete Honeycutt's pickup seat. I'll bet her bra spends more time on the danged gear shift than it spends on her.

BILLY BOB. (*Shocked.*) Lu Ann Hampton! You know that ain't true.

LU ANN. It is so, too. I seen 'em when they was parked out to the drive-in and she was danged near naked.

BILLY BOB. I never saw nuthin'.

LU ANN. 'Course you never saw nuthin'. You was too busy watchin' the movie. Mah Gawd, you was more worried about old Gary Cooper than Grace Kelly was.

BILLY BOB. Ah liked that movie.

LU ANN. Boy, you shore did.

BILLY BOB. Well, ah did.

LU ANN. No wonder Ruthie Lee has so many chest colds in the wintertime.

BILLY BOB. If Pete and Ruthie Lee was actin' like the way you said, that jest means they don't have any respect for each other.

LU ANN. Or for Gary Cooper.

BILLY BOB. Reverend Stone says that goin' on like that is a sinful sign of no respect.

LU ANN. Oh, brother.

BILLY BOB. People that behave thataway out to drive-ins and such-like is behavin' plumb un-Christian.

LU ANN. Well, at least they were sharin' somethin' more than a danged ol' box of popcorn.

BILLY BOB. A true Christian is pure in mind and body.

LU ANN. I wish you'd stop preachin', Billy Bob. Mah Gawd, ever'time we have somethin' important to discuss, you come up with a danged sermon.

BILLY BOB. What in the world are we discussin' that's important?

LU ANN. Your daddy's step-down Hudson Hornet, that's what!

BILLY BOB. My daddy's . . . For cryin' out loud, Lu Ann, sometimes you drive me absolutely nuts!

LU ANN. Well, you don't have to yell, Billy Bob.

BILLY BOB. Ah told you, an' told you, an' told you that we cain't have the Hudson.

LU ANN. Well, why not?

BILLY BOB. 'Cause my daddy's got to go over to Big Spring!

LU ANN. Well, it seems plumb funny to me that your daddy picked the very day of the senior picnic to go over to Big Spring. Ah mean, doesn't he know that the senior picnic is jest about the most important event in our whole schoolin' career?

BILLY BOB. Ah don't know if he does or not, he jest . .

LU ANN. Don't hardly seem fair to look forward to somethin' all these years only to have your daddy come along and mess it up.

BILLY BOB. Daddy ain't messed up nothin', he jest . . .

LU ANN. He's only doin' it for spite, Billy Bob.

BILLY BOB. No, he ain't, he's jest . . .

LU ANN. And spite in my book is jest plain sinful and un-Christian. (*She turns to go.*) Good night, Billy Bob.

BILLY BOB. (*Grabbing her arm.*) Now wait a minute, Lu Ann. (*They are very close now.*) Oh, boy, uh, uh. Ah will talk to Dad tonight and ask for the car again, okay?

LU ANN. Swell, Billy Bob. (*She kisses him.*) Good night, now.

BILLY BOB. Good night. By gollies, Lu Ann, ah'm gonna make danged sure we git that car.

LU ANN. Fine.

BILLY BOB. Danged sure! (*He exits.*)

(Lu Ann *watches him for a moment and then enters the house.*)

CLAUDINE. (*Entering, singing.*) "Don't let the stars get in your eyes." Well, mah, mah, look who's here. Billy Bob Wortman walk you home?

LU ANN. Yep.

CLAUDINE. Kiss him good night?

LU ANN. Maybe.

CLAUDINE. Well, ah'm glad your daddy never lived to see the day when his only little girl would be standin' on the front porch smoochin' with one of them worthless Wortman boys.

LU ANN. Oh, Ma.

CLAUDINE. 'Specially one with green hair.

LU ANN. How do you know? You peeked!

CLAUDINE. Didn't done it! It's all over Bradleyville how them ignernt basketball boys poured green dye or somethin' all over their empty heads.

LU ANN. Pete Honeycutt put 'em up to it.

CLAUDINE. That figgers. All them Honeycutts are crazy. God, ah remember once when Pete's *daddy* and me—oh, well, shoot, never mind. See your brother today?

LU ANN. Naw, he said he was goin' to come over to the school but he never.

CLAUDINE. Yeah, well, ah speck he's off runnin' around some place. Lordy, but he worries me, seems like ever since he come home from Korea he's been rollin' around like a tumbleweed. Foolin' around all day long in Sweetwater or Big Spring and drinkin' all night over to Red Grover's bar. All that drinkin' is no good for him, Lu Ann. If he keeps it up he's gonna wind up in the alcohol ward in the state hospital jest like his cousin Wilbur Bentley, you mark mah words. (*Lights up cigarette.*)

18

LU ANN. Aw, Ma. Nuthin' like that's gonna happen to Skip.

CLAUDINE. Lord, ah hope not. (*She settles into the armchair.*) Ahh, boy, well now, tell me about the assembly.

LU ANN. Ain't much to tell.

CLAUDINE. Ain't much to tell! Well, if that don't beat all, here you been runnin' around all week talkin' about that-there assembly, and when ah ask you about it, you up and say, "Ain't much to tell."

LU ANN. Oh, gawlee, Ma, it was the same old stuff, dull dull, dull.

CLAUDINE. Whattayou mean dull, dull, dull?

LU ANN. Oh, you know, first Mr. Palmroy got up and said how the Class of 1953 was one of the best ever at Bradleyville High. Then he had all the teachers stand up and he said how good they were; boy, ah had to laugh at that, but anyway, we gave 'em a big cheer. Then he introduced old Miss Millikan, who's gonna retire this year.

CLAUDINE. Bes Millikan! Retirin'!

LU ANN. Yep, after forty years! Can you imagine?

CLAUDINE. Mah God, Bess Millikan was my English teacher too, twenty-three years ago. Why she musta been a young woman at the time, but even back when we called her "old Miss Milikan."

LU ANN. Well, I cain't imagine her as ever bein' young, gawlee!

CLAUDINE. No, I don't guess anybody ever did. I spoze that's why she was always *Miss* Millikan. I hope you-all had a nice goin'-away for her.

LU ANN. Why, we shore did. Floyd Tatum came out and gave her an orchid.

CLAUDINE. Good.

LU ANN. Then Coach Charlton gave her a letter sweater of her very own to wear to the games.

CLAUDINE. A what?

LU ANN. A letter sweater, with a real Bradleyville letter on the front and a big number 40 on the back. She was gonna give a speech, but she started to cry of course, so we give her a big cheer and she sat down.

CLAUDINE. Why, the poor thing. I feel kinda sorry for her.

LU ANN. Well, I don't see why. Look at all them nice things she got.

CLAUDINE. I know, I know—but even so, it seems—oh, never mind. What happened next?

LU ANN. Then Coach Charlton read off the list of the basketball team and how we almost won district and ever'thing, and then bang, open come the gym doors and here comes the team onto the floor—with green hair! It looked like the Martians had landed or somethin'. Ever'body just hollered and carried on like idiots. We were havin' all kinda fun until stuffy old Mr. Palmroy had us sing the school song and we all went to our classes.

CLAUDINE. Well, it sounds like quite a time.

LU ANN. Uh-huh. But that wasn't the best part. When the noon hour came around, all of us girls that go with the basketball boys pretended that we didn't want to be seen with them.

CLAUDINE. You didn't!

LU ANN. Shore we did. Whenever they'd come around we'd run off. Billy Bob was runnin' after me and fell down into a great old big bunch of tumbleweeds.

CLAUDINE. That figgers.

LU ANN. Pete Honeycutt chased Ruthie Lee Lawell up and down the hall makin' funny noises.

CLAUDINE. Mah, mah, well, you best enjoy yourself while you can, honey, remember that your schoolin' days are the happiest days of your life.

LU ANN. Oh pooh.

CLAUDINE. Don't "oh, pooh" me, Miss Snippy Face. Ah know what ah'm talkin' about.

LU ANN. Well, if this is the *happiest* time of mah life, ah'm jest not too all fired shore ah want to go on livin'. Gee whiz.

CLAUDINE. You'll eat them words one of these days, believe you me.

LU ANN. What's so doggone happy 'bout dumb old school? I was sittin' there in study hall the other day and I got to lookin' at a picture there on the wall of one of them castles they got over there to Europe and way up in the top part of it was this little tiny door and I got to thinking to myself, boy, what I wouldn't give to git outta here for a spell and go over yonder to where that castle is. Climb up there and open that little door and look out at the trees and gardens and such like and holler out, "Hey, ever'body, look here, look at me. I've just opened the little door that's at the top of the whole wide world!

CLAUDINE. Well, ah don't know what me and your daddy did wrong in this life to produce such balloon-headed babies. Why weren't you workin' on your lessons 'stead of sittin' there dreamin' up fool notions?

LU ANN. 'Cause ah'm sick and tired of school, that's why! Boy, will I be happy to get out of there. Dumb old Mr. Palmroy grouchin' around and dumb old Mrs. Willis in dumb old biology class. "Learnin' the ways and means of the life of the plants has importance to learnin' the ways of our fellow human creatures." Boy, ah have to laff at that, I tell you.

CLAUDINE. Well, ah don't know . . .

LU ANN. It's dumb.

CLAUDINE. Well, ah don't know . . .

LU ANN. What's a plant got to do with people? Plants jest sit around doin' nuthin'. Gee whiz.

CLAUDINE. Some plants are mighty pretty.

LU ANN. Do you know that there are plants in this world that eat people?

CLAUDINE. Did Mrs. Willis tell you that?

LU ANN. No, she did not. Ah happen to know *that* for a fact.

CLAUDINE. Well, ah don't believe a word of it.

LU ANN. It's the Gawd's truth. Billy Bob and me jest happened to see a picture out to the drive-in that told us all about it.

CLAUDINE. A movin' picture! That's jest all made-up stuff.

LU ANN. This movie jest happened to be based on actual incidents!

CLAUDINE. Oh pooh.

LU ANN. These fellers went plumb up the Amazon River in a great old big canoe jest to find and film these man-eatin' plants.

CLAUDINE. What'd them man-eatin' plants look like?

LU ANN. They had these big red claw-lookin' outfits that grabbed on to you, you see; then there was this clackity, clackity kind of a noise and *gulp*, that's all she wrote.

CLAUDINE. You're makin' this all up.

LU ANN. Ah am not.

CLAUDINE. You are so, too. You and Billy Bob Wortman ain't **never** seed a movie out to that drive-in in your life.

LU ANN. What are you talkin' about, we go out there most ever' Satti-day night.

CLAUDINE. Not to watch no movie you don't.

LU ANN. Do too!

CLAUDINE. Don't either! You all go out there to smooch and fool around.

LU ANN. Nasty mind.

CLAUDINE. Nothin' nasty 'bout the truth. Ah don't know why they bother to show a movie at all. They oughter jest line up them pickup trucks and turn the *lights* out for a couple of hours.

LU ANN. Lot you know 'bout it.

CLAUDINE. Ah know a lot more than you think. Hangin' around at the drive-in, dreamin' 'bout castles in the air. Honey, you gotta start some serious thinkin' 'bout after you graduate. Now, are you and Ruthie Lee still wantin' to go to that business college in Big Spring?

LU ANN. Business college? My Gawd, Mama, I'm not goin' through all the trouble of gittin' outta one school jest to turn around and walk right into another one.

CLAUDINE. Well, then how 'bout gittin' you that summer job with me at the hospital? It's the best trainin' in the world if you're goin' to go on and be a nurse.

LU ANN. Oh, ah don't know, Mama. Ah don't want to think about it jest yet.

CLAUDINE. Well, you gotta think about it some time.

LU ANN. Ah jest wanna *go*, go anywhere. Outta this house, outta this town, plumb outta the state somewhere.

CLAUDINE. Jest wantin' to go ain't gonna git you anyplace. You gotta plan and work and know where you're goin'.

LU ANN. Ah know, ah know!

CLAUDINE. You know, you know! What do you know?

LU ANN. Ah *know* ah don't want to be stuck all mah life in a little old dried-up West Texas town, emptyin' bedpans at the god-damned hospital, like somebody ah *know!!*

CLAUDINE. (*Looks at her a moment, slightly taken aback by the outburst, then she sighs and slowly shakes her head.*) Ah gotta be gittin' on down to work now. Ah got all the fixin's laid out for you in the kitchen. When your brother gits home, you go ahead and cook the supper, will you?

LU ANN. (*Very low.*) Ah'm sorry, Mama.

CLAUDINE. And if you got schoolwork to do, git it done and don't spend the live-long night playin' that durn radio.

LU ANN. Okay, Mama.

CLAUDINE. (*Going out the door.*) See you later. (*As she exits*) Confounded kids. (*Lu Ann goes straight to the radio and clicks it on. A Western song twangs softly into the room. She starts to dance. The phone rings.*)

LU ANN. Comin'. (*She turns down the radio and picks up the receiver.*) Hello . . . Oh, hi, Eveline . . . Nothin', what are you doin'? . . . Chapter 4? Nope, ah haven't read it yet . . . Oh pooh on old Mrs. Willis . . . Of course ah'm goin' to the senior picnic . . . You still goin' with Floyd Tatum . . . You-all made up, huh . . . Of course ah'm goin' with Billy Bob, who'd you expect, Milo Crawford? (*She giggles.*) He's got so many blackheads he looks like a pepper shaker . . .

(*There is a loud crash outside and we hear Skip's voice offstage.*)

SKIP. Goddamnit to hell!

LU ANN. Ah gotta go now, Eveline, ah think ah hear mah brother comin' in. See you later, kid, 'bye. (*She hangs up the phone, turns off the radio, and hurries into the kitchen just as Skip stumbles onto the porch. He is followed by Dale Laverty. He is dressed in the traditional uniform of West Texas—white shirt, Levi's, cowboy boots, and straw Western hat. Dale Laverty is a great, honest, shambling sort of fellow. He wears a rumpled, cheap tan suit.*)

SKIP. Come on in this house, Dale Goddamnit, come on in. Ma! Lu Ann!

22

Where the hell is ever'body? Sit down, Dale. Ma, where the hell are you?

LU ANN. (*Entering from kitchen.*) Ma's gone down to work.

SKIP. The devil you say. You gittin' the supper?

LU ANN. Yes, ah am.

SKIP. Then to hell with it. (*To Dale.*) She couldn't boil a Vyenna sausage.

LU ANN. Well, so much for you then. (*She turns to go back into the kitchen.*)

SKIP. Now hold on a minute, damnit. Ah want you to meet somebody. Dale Laverty, this here is mah little sister, Lu Ann.

DALE. Howdy.

LU ANN. Hello.

SKIP. Dale drove over from San Angelo to visit me today, ain't that somethin'. We was in the same outfit in Korea.

LU ANN. Oh, is that right?

SKIP. Damn right, blastin' them gooks. Old Dale was hell on wheels with a B.A.R., regular John Wayne. Right, Dale?

DALE. Ah never done much really.

SKIP. Never done much! Why, hell's fire, boy, what you talkin' about? Did you know that this-here boy, he, he, uh, saved mah life over there in Korea?

LU ANN. (*Interested.*) Really?

SKIP. Damn right.

DALE. Aw hell, Skip.

SKIP. Saved your brother's butt, that's what he did. Wanna hear about it?

LU ANN. Lemme turn down the oven and put the salad back in the icebox first.

SKIP. You go ahead and do that little thing, honey.

(*She exits.*)

DALE. (*Going up to Skip.*) Gawlee, Skip, what are you tryin' to do, ah never saved your life or nuthin'.

SKIP. Shore, shore, I know. So what, we'll jest have some fun with little sister, okay?

DALE. Well, shore, ah guess.

SKIP. Whattayou think of Lu Ann—nice, huh?

DALE. (*Sincerely.*) She's real pretty.

SKIP. Yes, she is. She's mah one-and-only sister and you are mah one-and-only buddy. Only buddy ah got in the whole lousy world.

DALE. Aw hell, Skip.

SKIP. The only one. You saw how them slobs down at Red's acted. Lived

23

in this lousy town all mah life, served mah stinkin' country in Ko-rea, and they wouldn't even buy me a lousy beer.

DALE. Aw come on, Skip, you know that ain't true.

SKIP. The hell it ain't.

DALE. You got lots of friends in this-here town. What about that-there lodge you joined the other day?

SKIP. The Knights of the White Magnolia? Hell, Dale, none of them fellers are friends of mine. Ah joined that-there lodge to get ahead in this town. Damn right, that lodge is jest a steppin'-stone, buddy. I've got ideas that's gonna put this little old town right on its ear.

DALE. By gollies, Skip, if anybody can do it, you can.

SKIP. You're damn right I can. I got plans, buddy, big plans. Remember Corporal Rosenberg?

DALE. Yeah. Old Four-Eyes, the motor-pool clerk.

SKIP. That's the guy. Well, he had two college degrees. That's right, *two*—an A.M. and a F.M., some damn thing like that. Well, one afternoon when we was havin' some beers over to the N.C.O. club, he told me that even with all his education he wished he had my common sense.

DALE. No kiddin'.

SKIP. That's right. You see, Dale, all them college chumps like Rosenberg is good for is like one thing at a time—you know. But common-sense guys like me can move around, ya see. We can be goin' with three or four deals at once. Hell's fire, ah got me a couple of real-estate ideas figgered out over to Sweetwater that are flat gonna make a bundle.

DALE. Gawlee.

SKIP. Damn right. And that ain't all. After ah talk to old man Cullers over to the bank, and git me a little capital together, ah'm really gonna put 'er in high gear. You see, Dale, I got all these-here opportunities right out in front of me. And ah got the common sense as how to move out and latch hold of 'em.

DALE. Yeah!

SKIP. But you gotta be careful, you know what ah mean?

DALE. Well, ah . . .

SKIP. You just cain't go rushin' straight into things like a damn fool. No, sir. You gotta move kindly easy-like. Keep your eyes open and slip around. In business you got to know ever' side of things affore you decide to pick up the cards.

DALE. Yeah, ah speck so.

SKIP. Did you know that ah wasn't back in this town of Bradleyville more than five minutes affore old Derwood Herring was over here wantin' me to go in with him in the Western Auto store?

DALE. Them Western Auto stores is damn-good outfits.

SKIP. Hell, yes, they are!

DALE. We got one over to San Angelo.

SKIP. You know what ah told him? I said, "Now look here, Derwood, I appreciate the hell outta you comin' over here." You see, Dale, in business matters you always gotta be polite. "But ah just ain't the kind of feller just to jump on into things this way. No, sir. Ah gotta put my mind to work on it. Look at ever' side of this here deal. Now, you jest come around again, say, in a month or two, and maybe ah can figger out somethin' for you."

DALE. What did he say to that?

SKIP. What could he say? Hell, Dale, Derwood ain't dumb. He knows the truth of things. He just sorter mumbled somethin' like "Well, all right, Skip, if that's how you feel." Then he got the hell out.

DALE. Did he ever come back?

SKIP. Naw. The back-stabbin' s.o.b. went straight over to Earl Parker's place and got him to go partners.

DALE. That was a damn dirty thing to do.

SKIP. Ah was glad, Dale, glad he done it. Who the hell would want to spend the rest of their life runnin' a Western Auto store for Christ's sake?

DALE. Them places ain't much account anyway.

SKIP. Hell, no, they ain't.

DALE. We got one over to San Angelo that ah never liked much.

SKIP. When these real-estate outfits work out, why in ten years or so ah'll not only own that damn Western Auto store but the whole damn block it's sittin' in.

DALE. You'll do 'er too, buddy!

SKIP. You see, Dale, time don't mean a damn thing in the business world. It's what you do with it that counts. How would you like to come over here someday and have old Skip drive you on down to the country club in his new Cadillac, sit around the bar over there with Floyd Kinkaid and all them rich bastards, and talk about oil wells and such like?

DALE. Boy, that would be somethin'.

SKIP. Cain't ever tell, buddy. Why, hell's fire, ah might even buy into that livestock-haulin' outfit you're fixin' to go to work for.

DALE. The Hubbard Brothers?!

SKIP. Hell, yes. Why not? You see, Dale, all ah gotta do is talk to old man Cullers over to the bank and then . . .

LU ANN. (Entering.) All done.

SKIP. Yeah, that's fine, Lu Ann. You see, Dale, all ah need is a little capital, then . . .

LU ANN. What about the story?

SKIP. What story?

DALE. 'Bout me savin' your life over to Ko-rea.

SKIP. What the hell you talkin' about?

DALE. You know that time when, uh . . . that story you was gonna tell Lu Ann there.

SKIP. Oh yeah, well, let's see now. Remember me writin' to you-all 'bout how I was drivin' them convoy trucks over there?

LU ANN. Shore do.

SKIP. Well, sir. There was that time when the Marines caught hell and was retreatin' from the Chosan reservoir. Remember readin' that in the newspapers?

LU ANN. Ah think so.

SKIP. Well, we was there! Old Dale and me, a-bringin' them boys down through the hills. Snow on the ground, cold as hell, and by God surrounded by the entire Chinese gook army.

LU ANN. Gawlee.

SKIP. Damn right. The hills was covered by them little slant-eyed bastards like by-God ants! There was five truckloads of us, you see, comin' down this little old dirt road. Cold as hell and dog-assed surrounded. Well, as you can see, we was in somethin' of a fix, but it looked like we was gonna make it out okay. When all of a sudden they come down on us with their heavy artillery. Wham, wham, wham! In nuthin' flat three of our trucks was nuthin' but smokin' ruin.

LU ANN. Smokin' ruin?

SKIP. That's right, smokin' ruin! Then it happened! Bang, they got me! Direct hit, right on my truck! The next thing I know, ah'm lyin' out in the snow with dead bodies of Marines all around me. Well, sir, ah figgered ah'd best git the hell outta there pronto. So ah got up to take off and that's when ah seed 'em comin'.

LU ANN. Who?

SKIP. Who?! The goddamned gooks, that's who! (*To* Dale) *Who!* (*Back to Lu Ann*) About fifty of 'em comin' like a bat out of hell over this little rise and ever' one of 'em comin' right at me, and ah knew, ah *knew* that ah was standin' there a dead man. Nuthin' ah could do but stand there and watch 'em git closer and closer. Then, then by God it happened!

LU ANN. What?

SKIP. Ah heard a noise behind me and here comes old Dale, drivin' with one hand and shootin' with the other. Cuttin' them gooks down like by-God weeds. He tossed down the B.A.R. and, openin' the door of the truck, reached out and picked me off the ground, threw me into the front seat, and gunned that old truck like Billy Jim hell over the hill and outta there.

LU ANN. Mah gosh.

SKIP. And for doin' that this-here boy was awarded one of the highest medals that this country's got. The Good Conduct Medal with bar.

LU ANN. Wow!

SKIP. Ol' Laverty butt, my best buddy.

DALE. Aw hell, Skip.

SKIP. Yes, sir, that is the man that is sittin' right next to you on the sofa. Old Laverty butt, mah best buddy. (*Suddenly* Skip *stands up and grasps his stomach.*) Oh God, ah feel it comin' on again.

LU ANN. What's wrong?

SKIP. It's either mah old war wound, or the malaria, or, or—

LU ANN. My God, Skip, what is it?

SKIP. Yes, that's it, ah'm sure that's it.

LU ANN. What?!

SKIP. Oh, gotta go tap this kidney or by God drown.

DALE. Aw hell, Skip. (Skip *laughs and exits. There is a silence as* Dale *and* Lu Ann *grope around for a thread of conversation. With great effort.*) So you're a cheerleader, huh?

LU ANN. What?

DALE. Uh—so you're a cheerleader, huh?

LU ANN. Oh, yes.

DALE. That's great.

LU ANN. It's lots of fun.

DALE. Ah'll bet.

(Lu Ann *offers tangerine—he declines.*)

LU ANN. You—uh—you play any ball over in San Angelo?

DALE. Football. Left tackle, that's on the line.

LU ANN. Yes. Ah know.

DALE. We had a good team. You remember Jack Mathis?

LU ANN. Ah don't think so.

DALE. Well, Jack Mathis was our quarterback and he went over to the A and M and made Honorable Mention All Southwestern Conference Second Team Defense Guard.

LU ANN. That's neat.

DALE. He's the State Farm insurance man in Big Spring now.

LU ANN. No kiddin'?

DALE. That's right. He's doin' real good. Got him one of them ranch-style homes.

LU ANN. Wow. Uh—whattayou gonna do now that your army is over and all that?

DALE. Oh, ah got me a job with the Hubbard Brothers.

LU ANN. (*Guessing.*) Truck drivin'?

DALE. Livestock haulers, West Texas and New Mexico. Ah start next week.

LU ANN. Ah see.

DALE. Because of mah army experience ah got me a rig right away. Most guys have to start off as a helper but ah got a rig of mah own right off. Yes, ma'am, big red Mack diesel with air horns and ever'thing. Boy, it's really somethin'.

LU ANN. Ah'll bet.

DALE. Purrs like a kitten. You wouldn't think an engine that big could sound so sweet. Boy, it's really somethin', and they give it to me right off, best old sweetheart in the fleet.

LU ANN. They probably heard about your medal and things.

DALE. (*Taken aback.*) Yeah . . . uh, these your school books?

LU ANN. Biology and history, ugh.

DALE. Boy, ah hated school.

LU ANN. My mama says it's the happiest time of your life. Ever hear anythin' so silly?

DALE. Ah cain't buy that.

LU ANN. Me neither.

DALE. Whattayou gonna do after you graduate?

LU ANN. Gee, ah don't know. Mama wants me to go on to nursin' school.

DALE. That's a good job for a girl.

LU ANN. Ah spoze.

DALE. Mah sister is a dental assistant.

LU ANN. That's a good job.

DALE. Sure is. She makes pretty good money. Her husband works at Hubbard Brothers too.

LU ANN. Really?

DALE. You bet! They got 'em one of those great old big house trailers.

LU ANN. That's neat.

DALE. Shore is. It's got a livin' room, bathroom, kitchen, the works, and the best thing about it is that if you git tired of bein' in one own you can jest hook 'er up and take off, nuthin' to it. Spoze you were livin' in Snyder or Abilene or somewhere and you wanted to move to Amarillo? Well, sir, you jest hook up and take off. Furniture, dishes, clothes, ever'thin', jest take off. Now that is the way to live!

LU ANN. Gosh yes.

DALE. You pull into one of them trailer parks, you see, an' they got ever'thang. Gas, water, washin' machines, swings, septic tanks, some even got swimmin' pools.

LU ANN. Swimmin' pools?

DALE. You bet, and grass and trees and flowers and collie dogs runnin' around.

LU ANN. Gee, it sounds like heaven.

DALE. Yeah.

(*Their eyes meet for a long moment. Skip re-enters.*)

SKIP. Whooee, did ah need that!

DALE (*Nervously.*) You shore were gone a long time.

SKIP. Well, you know how it is, kid. The longer it is, the longer it takes. You-all gittin' along okay?

DALE. Sure, Skip. Jest fine.

SKIP. Well, now, ain't that real nice. You know, Dale, one of these days old Lu Ann is gonna make some lucky guy one helluva nice wife.

LU ANN. Aw shoot.

SKIP. Whattayou think, old podnah?

DALE. Ah truly believe she will.

SKIP. Damn right. But ah gotta tell you one thing right off. You got competition, boy.

DALE. Ah do?

SKIP. You better believe it. Old Lu Ann's got her a basketball-playin' dude. How many points Billy Bob score agin Snyder, Lu Ann?

LU ANN. Six.

SKIP. You hear that, Dale? Six big ones! God A mighty, what an eye, makes old Bob Cousy look like an amateur.

LU ANN. Billy Bob was doggone good over there to Snyder.

SKIP. Yeah, boy, and a lover too. I hear tell that Lu Ann kissed him so hard the other night that his hair turned as green as alfalfa.

DALE. Sounds like a helluva guy.

SKIP. Damn right! They tell me that when old Billy Bob grows up he's gonna rent his head out to pasture.

LU ANN. (*Playfully hitting at him.*) Oh, you. Now you quit pickin' on Billy Bob, he's a nice boy.

SKIP. Shore he's a nice *boy*, but maybe it's about time you started thinkin' about a nice *man*. An adult, grown-up man, 'stead of some pimply-faced, nose-pickin' kid. Somebody that can shake them bed springs till your toes curl up and you teeth rattle.

LU ANN. (*Holding her hands over her ears.*) Ah ain't gonna listen no more.

SKIP. Listen to what? Hell, ah never said nuthin'. Hey, Dale, you remember them wooden beds they had in that whorehouse in Tokyo?

DALE. (*Embarrassed and uncomfortable.*) No, Skip, ah, uh, don't, uh, remember.

LU ANN. Ah wish you wouldn't always talk dirty thataway.

29

SKIP. Who's talkin' dirty? Them wooden beds is a by-God historical fact. We was talkin' about 'em over to mah lodge meetin' the other night, Dale, and old L. D. Alexander said . . .

LU ANN. Boy, that figgers. Bunch of dirty-minded old men.

SKIP. What do you mean, "dirty-minded old men"? It jest so happens that some of the most important men in this town are members of the Knights of the White Magnolia.

LU ANN. That ain't the way ah heard it.

SKIP. What ain't the way you heard it? It's the by-God truth. Ain't that right, Dale?

DALE. Well, gawlee, Skip, ah don't know.

SKIP. (To Lu Ann.) You see there?

LU ANN. Sara Beth Phelps was over here the other day and told Mama that she didn't like for Rufe to go to them meetin's 'cause nobody does nuthin' but drink whiskey, play dominoes, and git into big fights.

SKIP. Well, what in the name of Jesus H. Christ does Sara Beth Phelps know anyway!

LU ANN. Rufe Phelps is a member, ain't he?

SKIP. Shore he's a member. That's why Sara Beth don't know a damn thing. 'Cause members ain't spozed to tell nobody, wives, or nuthin', what goes on in our meetin's.

LU ANN. How's come?

SKIP. How's come? 'Cause it's secret, that's how's come! We do lots of secret important things.

LU ANN. Shore, shore, like talkin' about wooden beds in Tokyo whore-houses.

SKIP. That was before the meetin', damnit, before the secret stuff. And who the hell ever taught you to say whorehouse! You tryin' to shame the family in front of company?

DALE. Ah, hell, Skip.

LU ANN. You jest said it yourself not two seconds ago.

SKIP. That don't mean you gotta go repeatin' it all over town. How about that, Dale? A little old fatty-legged high-school girl goin' around sayin' dirty words in her own by-God house. Ah don't know what the goddamned world's comin' to.

LU ANN. Pickin' on me ain't gonna change a thing. Ever'body in town knows that that-there lodge ain't worth a hill of beans and you're just puttin' a lot of stock into somethin' that ain't nuthin' at all.

DALE. (Getting up.) Well, ah speck ah better . . .

SKIP. That lodge is jest a steppin'stone, a steppin'stone, that's all!

LU ANN. Uh-huh. (She mimes crossing a stream.) Step, step, kerplunk!

SKIP. Come on, Dale, let's git the hell out of here and go on back to Red's place!

DALE. Well, uh, shore . . .

LU ANN. Mama says, if you keep hangin' out over to Red's place, you're gonna wind up bein' just like Wilbur Bentley.

SKIP. Well, ah don't give a damn if ah do. At least in the alcohol ward ah won't be pestered to death by a big-mouthed little sister. Now come on, Dale, let's go!

DALE. You go ahead, Skip! Ah'll be right with you.

SKIP. (*Exiting.*) Pick on a feller's lodge. Might as well pick on his country or his flag or somethin'. No damn respect, that's the trouble. No by-God respect. (*He exits. There is a moment of silence.*)

DALE. Old Skip's a lotta fun, ain't he?

LU ANN. Sometimes.

DALE. Lot of that stuff he said earlier he didn't really mean.

LU ANN. Oh, well, ah don't reckin it matters.

DALE. Listen, do you think it would be okay if ah called you some time? Ah mean, uh, you and that feller of yours ain't engaged or nuthin', are you?

LU ANN. Oh, shoot, no, we jest kinda go with each other, you know.

DALE. Shore. Well then, would it be okay?

LU ANN. What?

DALE. If ah maybe could call you or somethin'?

LU ANN. Oh, sure, Dale, that would be real neat.

DALE. Okay, by golly, ah'll jest do that. Real soon.

LU ANN. Swell.

DALE. Well, uh, so long.

LU ANN. So long. See you soon. (*Dale exits. She watches after him for a moment and then crosses into the room. She stands for a moment at the radio.*) Dale Laverty—Dale Laverty, gee, that's a pretty name. (*She switches on the radio, Western music booms forth as the act ends.*)

Set for Act Two of the Dallas Theater Center production of "Lu Ann Hampton Laverty Oberlander." Designed by Mary Sue Jones.

ACT II

The act takes place in 1963 in Red Grover's bar. A small, dim, beer-smelling West Texas dive. Lots of beer advertisements on the wall. Coors, Lone Star, Pearl, Miller's, etc. A small wooden bar, couple of tables and chairs. A beat-up jukebox. Above the bar is a large sign: WE RESERVE THE RIGHT TO REFUSE SERVICE TO ANYONE. RED's place has seen a lot of beer-swilling, head-knocking, gut-rumbling life and looks it.

As the scene opens we find Red Grover standing behind the bar, glumly watching Rufe Phelps and Olin Potts play checkers.

RUFE. Watch out there, watch out what you're doin' there!

OLIN. Hell, Rufe, it's mah move.

RUFE. Ah know it's your blamed move. But you cain't move mah checkers. Only yours.

OLIN. Ah ain't movin' yours, only ones ah'm movin' is the black uns.

RUFE. Your finger touched that checker right there and that checker is by God red.

OLIN. Mah finger never touched nuthin'. All ah'm movin' is the black uns.

RUFE. Red seen it. Hey, Red, didn't he touch this-here checker?

RED. Who gives a damn.

OLIN. Ah never touched nuthin'!

RUFE. Did so too!

OLIN. Didn't never either!

RUFE. Done it!

OLIN. Didn't!

RED. For Christ's sake! If you two cain't play that damned game without fightin' about it, then you can by God get the hell outta here.

RUFE. Well, hell, Red, he cheated.

OLIN. Ah never neither.

RED. (*Quietly.*) Ah ain't gonna tell you two again.

RUFE. Ah'm tired of playin' anyway.

OLIN. That's 'cause you're losin'.

RUFE. Shore ah'm losin'. How can anybody win with you a-movin' any damn checker on the board that pleases you?

OLIN. Ah'm only movin' the black uns!

RUFE. Ah never seen nuthin' like you, Olin Potts! Cheat at horseshoes, cheat at checkers, cheat at dominoes, cheat at ever'thang!

OLIN. Ah never cheat at nuthin'! And you know it!

RUFE. Never cheat? How 'bout the last time we went bowlin'. Hey, Red, he knocked down the by-God pin boy and called it a spare.

OLIN. Well, hell, ah figgered he should count for somethin'; 'sides that, a movin' target's harder to hit.

RUFE. (To Red.) You see there?

RED. Boy, you two are somethin' else. Anybody want another beer?

RUFE. Naw. Ah'm already gittin' the bloats.

RED. How about you, Olin?

OLIN. Two's mah limit, Red.

RED. (Mimicking.) "Two's mah limit, Red." Some customers. Sit around here all day long and buy four lousy beers.

RUFE. Ah cain't help it if beer bloats me.

RED. Well, damnit, drink somethin' else!

RUFE. Ah don't like nuthin' else.

RED. Oh, for Christ's sake.

RUFE. What are you-all so all-fired peckish about, Red? Me and Olin never drink more than four beers, ain't that right, Olin?

OLIN. Two's mah limit.

RED. Jesus Christ, some business ah got here. Bloated checker players all day long and by-God drunken maniacs at night.

RUFE. You're talkin' about Skip Hampton, ain't you?

OLIN. What's old Skip done now?

RUFE. Didn't you hear about what he did?

OLIN. Hell no, ah never hear about nuthin'.

RED. Stupid bastard tried to kill himself in here last night.

OLIN. Kill himself!

RED. That's right.

RUFE. Had him a knife, didn't he?

RED. Hell, no. The crazy son-of-a-bitch cut his throat with a broken bottle.

OLIN. Cut his throat! Well, whattayou know about that.

RED. Damnedest thing ah ever saw in mah life.

OLIN. What the hell happened?

RED. He came in here about, oh, 2:30 or 3:00 yesterday afternoon, lookin' like hell as usual, and started chuggin' down the old Thunderbird wine. Come about 8:00 he's drunk as billy hell and starts to mouth off again about Ko-rea.

OLIN. Oh, God, not again.

RED. That's right, them same old sad-assed stories. Well, sir, Pete Honey-cutt was standin' here at the bar and he turns over to Skip and says, "Why don't you shove it, Hampton—nobody wants to hear that old crap any more— Hell, that damned war's been over for *ten years.*"

OLIN. What did he do then?

RED. Well, sir, old Skip looks up and says, "You're a goddamned liar." That's right, jest as cool as you please. "You're a god-damned liar."

OLIN. Skip said that to Pete Honeycutt. My God, what did Pete do?

RED. Hell, you know old Pete Honeycutt, nobody calls him a liar. The next thing I know he's got Skip by the shirt front and slammed up into the corner. "Listen, you sad sack of crap," he says, "this is nineteen and goddamned sixty-three—you ain't no Korean hero no more—you're nuthin' but a stinkin' wino bum, the goddamned town joke!" Then he spins him around and kicks him in the ass. Knocked him right up agin the bar here.

RUFE. God Almighty.

RED. Well, sir, Skip gits up real slow like and ah figger he's gonna tangle with old Pete.

OLIN. Did he?

RED. Hell, no. He jest stood there lookin' at Pete for a second and then he started to cry.

RUFE. He did what?

RED. He started bawlin'. Damnedest thing ah ever seen. Stood there like a damned fool and cried like a baby.

OLIN. Whattayou know about that.

RED. Hell, ah liked to died laughin'. The whole place nearly come apart, old Pete jest doubled up and hollered. Jesus, it was funny! Then, by God, while we was laughin' there at him he reached behind him, got this-here beer bottle, broke it on the bar, and pulled the edge across his throat.

RUFE. My God!

RED. Hell, ah thought he was sure-enough dead. Ah mean, the blood jumped clean across the room. It's a damn good thing old Doc Crowley was across the street there to the Dixie Dinette or Skip would be on a slab at Strong's Funeral Home 'stead of the hospital. By God I've seen some pretty wild things in this dump, but last night takes the blue goddamned ribbon. Ah was moppin' up blood and broken glass for an hour.

OLIN. By gollies, ah don't know. It seems to me that ever since our lodge broke up, old Skip's jest sorter gone on downhill.

RED. That's bullshit! Skip Hampton was born goin' downhill, that stinkin' little lush is nuthin' but a washout and a loser.

RUFE. You know the one ah feel sorry for is his mother.

OLIN. Damn right, it's a shame that a fine woman like Claudine Hampton has got a burden like that on her.

RUFE. Two burdens, you're forgittin' about Lu Ann.

RED. Lu Ann, now there's a hot little number for you. (*He chuckles.*) Tough as a damned boot.

RUFE. That girl's plum wild now, that's a by-God fact.

OLIN. Well, ah don't know.

RUFE. You don't know! Why, hell, Olin, she's been movin' through this town like a tornado ever since she got shed of that husband of hers four or five years ago and moved back from over there to Snyder.

OLIN. Well, ah know all that, but hell, Rufe, she jest blows off a little steam now and again. She ain't *bad* or nuthin' like that.

RUFE. Any woman that would sit around a bar like this-here one drinkin' beer and smokin' cigarettes with a bunch of old hard-headed men is by God down in mah book as *bad!*

RED. Now hold on there, you're talkin' about some of my best customers.

OLIN. By God, Rufe, you got you a plum narrow mind, ah'll be damned if you don't—

RUFE. Now jest what the hell do you mean by that!

RED. He's tryin' to tell you that you're skinny-brained, Rufe.

RUFE. Who's skinny-brained?

OLIN. You are, that's who, you got a skinny brain in a big fat head!

RED. (*Laughing.*) That's tellin' him, Olin.

RUFE. (*Leaping up.*) By God, Olin, now you've gone too damn far. (*He assumes an old-time fighting stance.*) Git up, git up, so's ah can knock you down.

RED. Attaboy, Rufe!

OLIN. Don't be a damned fool, Rufe, sit down and forget it.

RUFE. Ah damned well won't forget it. Now, by God, Olin, git up and fight.

RED. Go ahead, Olin, you can take him.

(*The door opens and Lu Ann enters. The years have hardened her prettiness into a tough, smooth gloss. Her figure is still excellent. She is drugstore pretty, cologne and lipstick pretty. She wears the white uniform of a beauty operator.*)

LU ANN. What the hell's goin' on in here?

RED. Come on in, Lu Ann, you're jest in time for the fight of the century. We got old Hurricane Skinny-Brain versus Two's-My-Limit Lewis.

LU ANN. My God, what are you and Olin fightin' about now, Rufe?

RUFE. Well, we, ah, er . . .

RED. Go ahead, Rufe, tell her.

OLIN. We was jest arguin' about a bowlin' score, Lu Ann, that's all.

36

LU ANN. Ah heard about you sports over to the Bradleyville Bowl. Still smackin' down the pin boys there, Olin?

OLIN. Got two last Wednesday.

LU ANN. Damn good goin'.

RUFE. You ought to see 'em jump around when old Olin gits up there—it's plumb comical.

LU ANN. Sounds like it. My gawd, Red, gimme a beer before ah flat dry up and die.

RED. Comin' up, Lu Ann! Whattayou doin' over here today? You and Maud Lowery have another fight?

LU ANN. Aw, that goddamned old bag! What she knows about bein' a beautician wouldn't stuff a horny toad's butt.

RED. Better watch your step, Lu Ann, or Maud's gonna fire you one of these days.

LU ANN. *Fire me!* That'll be the goddamn day. Maud Lowery's Bon-Ton Beauty *Saloon*, for Christ's sake. There ain't a woman in this town comes into that shop wantin' anyone else to do their hair but me. Maud Lowery gits her hands on you and you walk out lookin' like a gunny sack. She couldn't curry a coyote and she's got the sand to call herself a beautician! Hell, ah studied beauty operation, Red, you know that. Probably could have had a shop of my own by now if it weren't for that worthless Dale Laverty.

OLIN. Where is old Dale now?

LU ANN. Who gives a damn. Why, I never hear from him any more, not since he pulled out on me one fine night with a gut full of hootch and snakes in his boots. Left me to bring up little Charmaine all by mahself.

RUFE. You're livin' with your ma now, ain't you, Lu Ann?

LU ANN. Yep, same old place. Mama helps me take care of Charmaine. She only works part time over to the hospital now.

RED. Been over to see your brother today?

LU ANN. Sure, sure, ah seen him.

OLIN. How's he gittin' along?

LU ANN. Well, Doc Crowley says he's goin' to be okay but ah don't know, he sure look peekity to me. Boy howdy, what a damn-fool thing to do

OLIN. Well, he'd had a lot to drink, ah spoze.

LU ANN. Skip always has a lot to drink. Maybe this will slow him down for a little while.

OLIN. (*Getting up.*) Well, ah gotta be gettin' back to the farm. Chores to do. (*To Rufe.*) You still wanna set that trotline in the mornin'?

RUFE. Hell, yes, I wanna set that line. I found a place out there on the lake that jest smells catfishy. Pick me up at the house about 4:30, okay?

OLIN. Will do. Well, ah'll see you-all later. (*He exits.*)

RUFE. So long, Olin.

LU ANN. You still workin' over to the refinery, Rufe?

RUFE. You bet. Same old job.

LU ANN. How's Sara Beth gittin' along these days?

RUFE. Well, she had the misery in her shoulder again last winter, but other than that she's all right, ah guess.

(*The door opens and Corky Oberlander enters. Corky is an open, friendly-type fellow in his mid-thirties. He wears khaki work clothes and a baseball cap.*)

CORKY. Howdy, Rufe.

RUFE. Hey there, Corky.

RED. Hey, Corky—whattayou say, boy?

CORKY. Don't say it, Red. How 'bout a beer?

RED. Comin' up.

CORKY. (*Spotting Lu Ann.*) Well, hello there, pretty girl. Hey, Red, who in the world is this pretty little thing?

RED. Lu Ann Laverty, Corky Oberlander.

CORKY. Well, I'm happy to meet you, Lu Ann Laverty.

LU ANN. Well, I'm happy to meet you, Corky Oberlander.

RED. Corky here is an inspector with the Highway Department.

CORKY. Yep, got transferred over here from Abilene. Didn't think I was going to like it much till now.

LU ANN. Aw hell.

CORKY. Care to join me at a table?

LU ANN. Suits me.

RUFE. Well, ah gotta be goin'.

RED. Take it easy, Rufe.

RUFE. If I'm late for supper, old Sara Beth will be mad as hell. (*He exits.*)

RED. You two want anythin' else?

CORKY. Nuthin' for me, thanks. (*To Lu Ann.*) *How about you?*

LU ANN. Naw, ah'm okay.

RED. That figgers. I'm gonna go out back and stack some cases. If anybody comes in, sing out for me, will you?

CORKY. Will do. (*Red exits. There is a long pause.*) Well, here we are.

LU ANN. Looks like.

CORKY. Want me to play the jukebox?

LU ANN. Naw, sometimes them damn twangy guitars git into my nose.

CORKY. Yeah, well. How come the white uniform—you a nurse or somethin'?

LU ANN. Nurse? Hell no, ah'm a beauty technician.

CORKY. No kiddin'.

LU ANN. That's right. Ah got me a diploma from the Sanford School of Beauty Culture over there in San Angelo.

CORKY. Well now, that's real fine.

LU ANN. Sure is. Ah went to night school, took me twelve whole months.

CORKY. Twelve months?

LU ANN. That's right. I probably could have finished a whole lot sooner if it weren't for that worthless Dale Laverty.

CORKY. Your husband?

LU ANN. Mah ex-husband. Ah'm divorced.

CORKY. Ah see.

LU ANN. You married?

CORKY. Ah was once.

LU ANN. What happened?

CORKY. Oh, ah don't know, Peggy Sue and ah jest never seemed to git along. Seemed like ever' time I was fixin' to move in, she was fixin' to move out. Never could get it together.

LU ANN. Boy, ah know what you mean there, buddy. With me and Dale it was trucks and trailer houses! You ever live in a goddamned trailer house?

CORKY. Nope.

LU ANN. Boy, you ain't missed nuthin'. Cramped, miserable little old tin-boxie outfits—burn up all summer and freeze off all winter. No room to do a damned thing in. Dale would blow a fart and my eyes would water for three days.

CORKY. Sounds like a helluva home life.

LU ANN. Oh, man, it was de-loox. Stay out at them damned trailer parks, might as well live on a tumbleweed farm. Two or three burnt-up little old trees, a couple of splintery teeter-totters, and five hundred rattlesnakes.

CORKY. Rattlesnakes?

LU ANN. You bet your life, *rattlesnakes!* Hell, they used to crawl up under that goddamned trailer house like they owned it.

CORKY. Jesus!

LU ANN. You said it, pal.

CORKY. Why the hell didn't you move into a real house?

LU ANN. Old Dale said he didn't want to be tied down. "Wanna be movin' around," he said, "free as a bird." Boy, there's a laugh for you. We moved from San Angelo to Snyder and that was it. That trailer sat in the Shady Grove Mobile Home Park until the tires rotted off. Hell's fire, that was no way to live. 'Specially after Charmaine come along.

CORKY. Charmaine?

LU ANN. Mah little *girl*. Ah didn't tell you ah had a little girl, did ah?

CORKY. No.

LU ANN. Well, she's just the prettiest little thang around, that's all. Good as gold, never no noise or trouble, no, sir, not even when she was a baby. Didn't even cry at night.

CORKY. Whattayou know.

LU ANN. Well anyways, here ah was stuck out at the Shady Grove in Snyder with a little baby girl to look after and nuthin' to do all day but hunt rattlesnakes with an O'Cedar mop.

CORKY. What was Dale doin' all this time?

LU ANN. Dale! Hell, he was always off deliverin' cattle for the goddamn Hubbard Brothers. Be gone weeks at a time in that damn truck of his. Then when he was home that's all he could talk about. Trucks. God, ah got sick of it. Kenworth, Mack, Reo, White, GMC, International, hell, you'd think they was Presidents of the United States or somethin'. I never went nowhere and he'd come home and gas about all the places he'd been. So one boozy evenin' when he was home lappin' up the Jim Beam and talkin' about the new shower baths at the Top of the World truck stop in Moriarty, New Mexico, ah went right through the roof. "Listen, you flap-mouthed son-of-a-bitch," ah said, "if that cattleshit-smellin' semi you got out in the yard there means more to you than me and li'l Charmaine, why don't you jest haul your butt into the cab and boom on outta here for good."

CORKY. What happened?

LU ANN. He did it! Slammed out of the trailer, ground about fourteen gears, knocked over the mailbox, ran over our mangy collie dog, and took off down the road. Never saw him again—he didn't even show up at the divorce trial.

CORKY. So you come on back here, huh?

LU ANN. Yep. Buried the dog, sold the trailer, picked up Charmaine, and come on home to Bradleyville.

CORKY. That's a damn shame.

LU ANN. What is?

CORKY. Your marriage breakin' up and all that.

LU ANN. Oh, hell, nuthin' to trouble yourself about. Ah think it was probably for the best.

CORKY. Think so?

LU ANN. Sure. Ah'm doin' okay. Got a good job over to the beauty shop, drink a few beers now and then, watch the television, you know.

CORKY. Shore, shore. Ever git the itch to go on any moonlight truck rides?

LU ANN. Long or short haul?

CORKY. Either way you want.

LU ANN. No, thanks. From now on, ah go by automobile or not at all.

CORKY. You're an automobile goer, are you?

LU ANN. Sometimes. What kinda car you got?

CORKY. Chivy.

LU ANN. What year?

CORKY. Bran'-new Impala.

LU ANN. Good model. Hey, remember when they had them step-down Hudson Hornets?

CORKY. Shore do.

LU ANN. There was a helluva car. The fella ah went with in high school had one of them. Boy, we went ever'where in that thang. Step down and saddle up.

CORKY. Lots of leg room, huh?

LU ANN. It was a damn-good car. Went to the senior picnic in that car. Jesus, you shoulda seen ever'body's head turn.

CORKY. Big day, huh?

LU ANN. The best. Gawd, ah'll never forgit it. Me and the captain of the basketball team in a great old big shiny Hudson. Hot damn!

CORKY. Well, ah never owned no Hudson, but ah did have me a Kaiser once.

LU ANN. A Kaiser!

CORKY. A Kaiser. A great old big Kaiser with a silver buffalo-head hood ornament.

LU ANN. God, them was ugly cars.

CORKY. Ugliest cars in the world. They ain't never made anythin' bigger and uglier than my old green Kaiser. Hell, ah bet that damn thing weighed five ton, got about two miles to the gallon, and burned more oil than the *Super Chief*. I had a wreck in that damn thing once—hit an Oldsmobile head-on.

LU ANN. What happened?

CORKY. Totaled that damned Olds, tore it to pieces. Put the block right in the back seat, and that Kaiser? One broken headlight. That's right, one broken headlight! That Olds was totaled and the Kaiser only had a broken headlight. That car was by Gawd built. Solid, you know.

LU ANN. They built 'em good back then.

CORKY. Damn right they did. A buddy of mine nearly killed me with that car one time.

LU ANN. How come?

CORKY. Well, we was goin' deer huntin' one year, me and a bunch of guys. Couple of us took a pickup and loaded ever'thin' in the back—the tent, the bedrolls, the rifles, some boxes of chow, all that crap, and took off, with the rest of the guys followin' in my Kaiser. Well, sir, we was movin' on down the road drinkin' six-packs of Pearl and generally jackassin' around when old Len Hanawald, who was drivin' my Kaiser, decided he'd race us. Hell, that car wouldn't do more than sixty goin' straight downhill, but old Len hit the horn and around us he comes. Well, sir, ah leadfooted that pickup and take him like he's standin' still—about a quarter of a mile down the road ah come to this intersection with a great old big stop sign lookin' right at me. So bein' a good citizen, ah screech to a halt. Ah no sooner get stopped when somethin' makes me look into the rear-view mirror and all ah can see is this silver buffalo comin' right at me. Ah mean, the whole rear-view mirror is nuthin' but a big silver buffalo. Next thing ah know, Len has piled into the back of the pickup at sixty fat miles an hour. Hell, we scattered bedrolls, .30-30's, and Campbell's pork and beans all over West Texas. Put mah head smooth through the windshield. Sixteen stitches.

LU ANN. Jeeezus!

CORKY. Knocked out all mah front teeth. These are false. Look real, don't they?

LU ANN. Shore do. Whatever happened to that car?

CORKY. The Kaiser? Oh, ah gave it to mah brother when ah went into the army and he tore it up some way.

LU ANN. That's a damn shame. You got a dime?

CORKY. Yeah. (*He gives her a dime, she plays the jukebox. Song comes on low.*)

LU ANN. Ah got a brother that's pretty good at tearin' up things too.

CORKY. Cars?

LU ANN. *Lives.*

CORKY. Lives!

LU ANN. That's right, pal, lives! His life, mah life, our mama's life. You recollect that king that ever'thin' he touched turned to gold?

CORKY. King Midas?

LU ANN. That's the dude. Well, mah brother, Skip, has a touch too, only ever'thin' he touches goes bad. Cain't hold no job, on the goddamn bum all the time, livin' off mama like a leech. Now he's flat on his can in the hospital with a cut throat.

CORKY. Was that your brother that did that?

LU ANN. That's the fella. Old playboy Skip. Anythin' for a laugh.

CORKY. Ah've never heard of such a thing. Cuttin' his own throat! Jesus, that makes me goose-pimply jest thinkin' about it. What's wrong with him, is he crazy or somethin'?

LU ANN. No. No, ah don't think Skip's crazy, he jest cain't seem to catch hold of anything, that's all—never seemed to get started. Never married, never held on to a job very long. Jest sorter hung around year after year boozin' it up and dreamin' up big plans.

CORKY. What kind of plans?

LU ANN. Oh, all kinds of plans. Catfish farmin', aluminum siding, uranium prospectin', real estate, anythin' that would make a quick buck. Hell's fire, he even went into the chinchilla business.

CORKY. Oh, good God.

LU ANN. Was gonna make a fortune. Built a bunch of cages in the storeroom and bought him some chinchillas. Nuthin' to it, he says. Feed 'em a little alfalfa and let 'em breed away.

CORKY. Sounds easy enough.

LU ANN. Oh, hell yes! He had 'em about a month when the first norther blew in. 'Course Skip was off drunk somewhere and didn't plug in the 'lectric heater he had in there to keep 'em warm, so they all froze. Poor little old things all humped up in them wire cages froze stiff. Skip came back home and tried to skin 'em, but it was too late then.

CORKY. What kinda work does your brother do now?

LU ANN. Pumps gas over to the Texaco station when he's sober. Aw, to hell with him. Tell me some more about yourself.

CORKY. Well, ah was over to . . . (*The door opens and* Milo Crawford *makes a furtive entrance. He glances nervously around.*)

MILO. Hello.

CORKY. Howdy.

LU ANN. Well, ah'll be damned. If it ain't old Milo Crawford.

MILO. Hello. Is, uh, is Red around any place?

CORKY. He's out back. (*Calling out.*) Hey, Red, you got a customer.

RED. (*From offstage.*) Tell him to keep his shirt on for a minute, damnit!

MILO. (*Very low.*) No hurry, Red.

LU ANN. Well, how you been there, Milo?

MILO. Oh, fine, jest fine.

LU ANN. Good.

(*There is a long pause while* Milo *bumbles around.*)

MILO. Ah beg your pardon, miss, but do ah know you?

LU ANN. Why, of course you do, Milo. My Gawd, we went to high school together.

MILO. Oh, ah see. (*He doesn't.*)

LU ANN. Ah was Lu Ann Hampton.

MILO. You mean you ain't any more?

LU ANN. Well, no, Milo, ah got married. Mah name is Laverty now.

MILO. Oh, ah see. (*He goes up to* Corky.) Is this Mr. Laverty?

43

CORKY. Mr. Laverty?!

LU ANN. Good God, Milo, git your head back in the socket! You still don't know me, do you?

MILO. Well, to tell the truth, no, ma'am, ah don't. But Mr. Laverty here looks kindly familiar.

CORKY. Goddamnit, ah ain't Mr. Laverty!

LU ANN. For Christ's sake, Milo, you ain't got the sense God gave a tumblebug.

RED. (*Entering.*) What can ah do for you . . . (*He spots* Milo.) What in the name of hell!

MILO. (*Grinning and fawning around.*) Howdy there, Red.

RED. Whattayou doin' in here, Milo, the church burn down or somethin'?

MILO. No, ah, nuthin' like that, Red.

RED. Uh-huh. You know, Milo, if your mama knew that you was in here, she'd flat bust a gusset. She ain't dropped dead or nuthin' like that, has she?

MILO. Oh no, Mama is in real fine health, thank you.

RED. Well, was there anythin' you wanted?

MILO. Oh, ah don't know. Let's see, uh, Miller, Schlitz, Bud, Pearl uh-huh. All them is kinds of beer ain't they?

RED. That's right, Milo.

MILO. Ah see. You don't sell Dr. Pepper, do you?

RED. No, Milo, we don't.

MILO. Well, then, uh, how about a pack of them potato chips?

RED. Comin' right up, Milo. That'll be fifteen cents.

MILO. They're only a dime over to the drugstore.

RED. Well, this ain't the goddamned drugstore! Now, do you want 'em or not?

MILO. Yes, sir.

RED. Well?

MILO. Well, what?

RED. Milo, don't tell me you have defied God, your mama, and the First Baptist Church to come in here and buy a damned pack of potato chips. Now what the hell else do you want?

MILO. Oh, ah come over here to see if you-all wanted to contribute to the Jaycees' Beautify Bradleyville Campaign.

RED. You're a Jaycee nowadays, are you, Milo?

MILO. Yes, sir, and ah am on the committee to visit the store owners and git them to make a contribution so's we can beautify Bradleyville.

LU ANN. You the same bunch of fellas that put the statue of Colonel Kinkaid in the city park?

MILO. (*With great pride.*) Yes, ma'am, that was us all right.

LU ANN. Ugliest damn thing ah ever saw in mah life.

RED. That damned statue is so ugly even the pigeons won't shit on it. What the hell you monkey nuts got in mind for beautiful this year, Milo?

MILO. The, uh, money goes to repair the cemetery wall.

RED. Oh, it does, does it.

MILO. Yes, the old one is a disgrace to the community. It's full of cracks and splotches and spidery things.

RED. Well, now ain't that a goddamned shame.

MILO. Yes, it is. (*He pulls out a small notebook.*) Now, what can ah put you down for?

RED. Nuthin'.

MILO. Nuthin'?

RED. That's right, pal, nuthin'. N-U-T-H-I-N. As far as ah'm concerned, that splotchy, cracked, old spidery wall is damned fine with me. It's got by God character. Lots more character than this damn town has. Bradleyville. Jesus, how ah ever wound up in this burnt-out collection of cowboys and tumbleweeds is beyond me. For two cents ah'd sell this damn dump and haul ass back to Meridian, Mississippi, where ah by God belong.

MILO. We'd sure hate to see you go, Red.

RED. Oh, hell, yes, you would. You and your mama and the rest of the damn Baptists would hold a regular wake if ah left, wouldn't you? Have a damn parade most likely, with all the goody-goodies on one side of the street and all the booze-soaked, beer-swillin', fat-gutted winos on the other. After ah'm gone, you-all can put up another statue in that patch of dirt you call a city park, make it even uglier than the one of that senile, old idiot Colonel Kinkaid. And on the base you can put this-here inscription, *Red Grover, he hated ever' minute of it.* Now, get on outta here, Milo. Ah'm tired of lookin' at you.

MILO. Well, gawlee, Red, ah . . .

RED. Now wait a minute, Milo. Come to think of it, there is somethin' you can do for me.

MILO. Why sure, Red. Ah'd be happy to do anythin' ah can.

RED. Well, sir, you go on back down to that Jaycee meetin' and tell them goddamned deadbeats to git over here and pay their goddamn beer tabs, and ah'll give you enough money to put up a splotchy wall plumb around the whole town of Bradleyville.

MILO. Well, that, uh . . . we, uh . . . they . . .

RED. Now git your ass outta here. Ah got work to do!

MILO. Ah'm goin', ah'm goin'. Ah guess ah better be goin'. It sure was nice to meet you, uh, Mr. and Mrs., uh . . .

CORKY. If you say *Laverty* ah'm gonna belt you!

MILO. Well, uh, no . . . Ah mean . . .

RED. Git outta here!

MILO. Well, it's shore been nice. (*Crosses back for potato chips.*)

RED. Git!

(Milo *exits in a hurry.*)

LU ANN. (*Laughing.*) Old Milo Crawford, by God, he ain't changed in ten years.

RED. (*Muttering.*) Bloated checker players, drunken maniacs, and by-God, bumble-dickin' Jaycees. (*He exits.*)

CORKY. Jest exactly what the hell was that, anyway?

LU ANN. That was a Milo Crawford.

CORKY. You got any more like that around this town?

LU ANN. Naw, old Milo's one of a kind, thank God.

CORKY. Oh, ah don't know. Mah boss over to Abilene would have run him a close second.

LU ANN. Is that a fact?

CORKY. Damn right. God, was ah happy to transfer out of there.

LU ANN. How long you been with the highway?

CORKY. 'Bout eight years.

LU ANN. Red says you're an inspector. What do you inspect?

CORKY. Dirt.

LU ANN. What kinda dirt?

CORKY. The kinda dirt they put on the highway affore they shoot asphalt all over it.

LU ANN. Uh-huh. What else?

CORKY. What else what?

LU ANN. What else do you do?

CORKY. That's it.

LU ANN. Just go around lookin' at dirt?

CORKY. What's wrong with that?

LU ANN. Well, I don't know, it jest seems kindly piddlin'.

CORKY. What do you mean, piddlin'? It's a damned important job.

LU ANN. What's so damned important about lookin' at dirt?

CORKY. (*Patiently.*) If the grade of fill underneath the asphalt isn't right, you get holes in the highway, that's what's so damned important about dirt.

LU ANN. Well, you must be doin' a pretty piss-poor job. Ever' god-damned highway in this state is as holey as Billy Graham's mother-in-law.

CORKY. Well, goddamn! What the hell do you know about anythin'. Goddamn beauty operator.

LU ANN. Beauty *technician*, you dumb, dirt-lookin' gourd-head!

CORKY. Dirt-lookin' gourd-head! By God, woman, you can git plumb nasty sometimes.

46

LU ANN. My mama once told me there was nuthin' nasty about the truth.

CORKY. Oh yeah? Your mama ever say anythin' about sittin' around beer bars and pickin' up strangers!

LU ANN. Pickin' up strangers! Ah'm not the one that walked in here and said, "Why, looky here, Red, who in the world is this pretty little thing?" Hell, that-there line went out with the by-God *zoot suit*.

CORKY. Yeah, well, ah guess ah jest ain't as up to date as the rest of your boyfriends in this dump.

LU ANN. They ain't so bad. Git your nose out of the asphalt someday and maybe you'll learn somethin'.

CORKY. Aw, to hell with it! (*He starts out.*)

LU ANN. Yeah, that's right, go on and go!

CORKY. I'm goin' all right, I'm goin' over to my place, take a shower, change clothes, crank up my old Chivy and come over to your place and take you out to supper.

LU ANN. You are?

CORKY. Damn right! Where do you live?

LU ANN. 301 North Grand.

CORKY. Seven okay?

LU ANN. Fine with me.

CORKY. Good. Ah'll see you at seven. We'll go over to Bob Spring.

LU ANN. Suits me.

CORKY. See you then. (*He starts to exit, then stops and turns.*) Oh, uh, wear somethin' pink, will you?

LU ANN. Pink! What the hell for?

CORKY. Ah like pink, it's a nice color.

LU ANN. Well la-de-da. Lemme tell you somethin', pal, old Peggy Sue mighta been a vision of loveliness in pink, but old Lu Ann in pink looks like somethin' you win at a carnival.

CORKY. Oh, well, hell with it, wear what you want then.

LU ANN. Thanks bunches.

CORKY. Seven, right.

LU ANN. Right. (*He exits. She stands watching the door for a moment, then calls out*) Hey, Red!

RED. (*Entering.*) Whattayou want?

LU ANN. What kinda name is Oberlander?

RED. Hell, I don't know. German?

LU ANN. Yeah, maybe so. Hum, Oberlander—Corky Oberlander, by gollies, that's a right pretty name, don't you think?

RED. Who gives a damn.

ACT III

The time is 1973 in the Hampton home. Few changes in the furnishings. New slipcovers, maybe, and a television set in place of the radio. The rabbit ears on top of the set are covered with aluminum foil.

As the scene begins, Charmaine *is lying on the sofa reading a magazine. She is the ACT I image of Lu Ann. Small, blonde, and pretty. She wears a mini-skirt and a sweater. Her transistor radio blares out rock music. The Upstage door opens and Skip appears. Time, wear, and booze have taken their toll of Skip. His hair has grayed, he wears thick glasses, and his hands shake. Across his neck is the scar from his suicide attempt, which he makes no effort to conceal. He wears a faded flannel shirt and oversized pants. He crosses to the table and sits down.*

SKIP. For Christ's sake, Charmaine, turn that damn thing off. My head's flat splittin' in two.

CHARMAINE. Aw, go to hell!

SKIP. Aw, please. My head hurts. Ah'm sick.

CHARMAINE. That's tough!

SKIP. I'm gonna tell your ma. Jest see if ah don't.

CHARMAINE. Who gives a damn.

SKIP. Aw, please. That noise is killin' me.

CHARMAINE. Oh, all right. (*Clicks off radio.*)

SKIP. How you kids can stand that noise is beyond me.

CHARMAINE. Maybe it's because we don't stay up all night messin' up our heads with fortified Thunderbird.

SKIP. I wasn't drinkin'! Ah ain't touched no wine in a long, long time.

CHARMAINE. Shore, shore.

SKIP. It's the God's truth.

CHARMAINE. Then how come you were in the bathroom all mornin' with your head in the commode. Hell, they could hear you gaggin' plumb over to Big Spring.

SKIP. A lot you know, a lot you know. When you drink for a long time and then stop, your stomach shrinks up and you get the mornin' sickness.

CHARMAINE. The mornin' sickness! You're crazy; the only people that gits the mornin' sickness is pregnant women.

SKIP. You're the one that's crazy. Pregnant women git the varicose veins, that's all.

CHARMAINE. The varicose veins?

SKIP. It's caused by lack of iron in the blood cells.

CHARMAINE. Boy, are you dumb—whoever told you that?

SKIP. Ah saw it on the television.

CHARMAINE. That's the dumbest thing ah ever heard.

SKIP. Ah saw it, ah tell you.

CHARMAINE. Oh, you never saw nuthin'. You were probably jest havin' them delirium tremors again.

SKIP. Ah ain't never had them things!

CHARMAINE. Oh no? What about the time you said the bullfrogs was after you.

SKIP. Ah don't remember nuthin' about it.

CHARMAINE. That had to be one of the funniest things ah ever seen in mah life. "Help, help, the whole house is full of bullfrogs."

SKIP. You're makin' this all up.

CHARMAINE. "Git 'em off me, git 'em off me! The whole house is full of bullfrogs!"

SKIP. Keep it up, Miss Smarty Pants, just go on and keep it up and ah'm gonna tell on you.

CHARMAINE. Who gives a hoot what you tell.

SKIP. I know somethin'. Boy, do I know somethin' on you.

CHARMAINE. You don't know nuthin' at all.

SKIP. Oh yes, ah do.

CHARMAINE. Oh—yeah, like what?

SKIP. Like what you and Charles Black was doin' out to Lake Bradley-ville last Saturday afternoon.

CHARMAINE. You weren't out there.

SKIP. Ah was so, too.

CHARMAINE. Weren't.

SKIP. Was too. Ah was helpin' old Bowdwin Cassidy out to his bait stand and ah seen you

CHARMAINE. Boy, what a big fat lie.

SKIP. It ain't either.

CHARMAINE. It just so happens that Charles and me was parked plumb across the lake from Bowdwin's bait stand, so you couldn't have seen a danged thing.

SKIP. Oh no? (*He mimes putting a pair of binoculars to his eyes.*) Peek-a-boo.

CHARMAINE. Do you mean to tell me that you and that damned smelly old Bowdwin Cassidy stood around and spied on Charles and me through binoculars!

SKIP. Gotcha there, don't I; boy, I really gotcha there.

CHARMAINE. Ah oughta slap your ears off you! You dirty old sneak.

SKIP. You better not try nuthin' like that or ah'll tell. Ah'll tell what me and Bowdwin seen.

CHARMAINE. Well, go ahead. Nobody's gonna believe an old busybody like Bowdwin, and ever'body knows you're crazy.

SKIP. Ah'm not neither.

CHARMAINE. Stupid as a cattle guard. Crazy Skip Hampton.

SKIP. You shouldn't oughta call me names that way.

CHARMAINE. Ever'body in town calls you them names—jest because you're my uncle, ah don't see why ah cain't. (Shouts out window.) Crazy Skip Hampton!

SKIP. Them people in town calls me them names 'cause they're skeered of me.

CHARMAINE. Skeered of you! Boy, that's a hot one. Man, there ain't nuthin' skeered of you.

SKIP. They are skeered of me 'cause ah have killed people.

CHARMAINE. Baloney!

SKIP. In the war, ah killed 'em in the war, lots of people!

CHARMAINE. Run for your lives, ever'body, here comes crazy old Skip.

SKIP. Don't say that! Lu Ann told you not to call me that no more.

CHARMAINE. And the Crazy Man Award of 1973 goes to Skip Hampton!

SKIP. I'm gonna tell your mama on you!

CHARMAINE. Why don't you tell my daddy, you and him was big pals in the Civil War or somethin', why don't you tell him?

SKIP. Ah don't know where he is any more. He used to come and visit me sometimes, but ah don't know where he is any more.

CHARMAINE. Well, ah know where he is. Ah went and seen him one time.

SKIP. Aw, you never either.

CHARMAINE. Ah did so, too! Ah heerd that he was workin' for Hubbard Brothers over to San Angelo, so ah got Charles Black to drive me over there and ah seen him.

SKIP. You shouldn't have done that.

CHARMAINE. Why not? Ah got a right to see mah own real daddy, ain't ah? Anyways, ah never talked to him or nuthin'. Ah jest had a feller point him out to me and ah seen him, that's all.

SKIP. How did he look?

CHARMAINE. Fat.

SKIP. Fat?

CHARMAINE. That's right. Old, fat, and kind of dumb-lookin', you know. God, what a letdown. Ah don't know what ah was lookin' for, but it damn sure weren't no dumb fat slob, leanin' up agin a smelly old semi smokin' a cigarette and probably thinkin' about nuthin' at all.

SKIP. Now, listen here, Charmaine. Dale was one damned good old boy and don't you forget it.

CHARMAINE. Don't forget it? Aw, cool it, Uncle Bullfrog, ah already have. (She goes back to her magazine. Lu Ann appears on the front porch carrying two large bags of groceries. Now in her late thirties, Lu Ann is stouter and mellowed. Her beauty is placid and matronly. She wears a white uniform with her name over the pocket, on the back of the uniform is a blue wagon wheel with Howdy Wagon printed around it.)

LU ANN. Somebody open the door.

CHARMAINE. (To Skip.) You do it.

SKIP. Do it yourself, smarty pants.

CHARMAINE. Go to hell!

SKIP. Same to you!

LU ANN. Somebody open this damn door!

SKIP. Okay, okay, ah'm comin'. (He opens the screen door.)

LU ANN. Thanks. (Crossing to kitchen.) Ah heard loud voices comin' outta here. You two ain't been fightin' again, have you? (She enters kitchen.)

SKIP. Ah'm gonna tell on you.

CHARMAINE. Who cares.

SKIP. You got that dress on she don't like.

CHARMAINE. So what!

LU ANN. (Entering room.) Whooee, ah'm bushed! Charmaine, get off your lazy can and put them groceries away.

CHARMAINE. Aw hell.

LU ANN. Git!

CHARMAINE. Oh, all right. (Getting up.)

LU ANN. What are you doin' with that damned mini-skirt on?

CHARMAINE. Ah'm only wearin' it around the house.

LU ANN. Well, you better. If ah catch you outside in that thing, ah'm gonna paddle somebody's mini butt!

CHARMAINE. Oh, God, Mama, you are absolutely crude. (She goes into the kitchen.)

LU ANN. Right on, sister! (She sits on the sofa and removes her shoes.) Oh, mah aching feet. Hell, ah bet we said howdy to fifteen new families today.

SKIP. Big Spring is shore gittin' big.

LU ANN. Shore is. You look in on Mama today?

SKIP. Yeah. She's okay.

LU ANN. Give her any dinner?

SKIP. Shore, shore.

LU ANN. Empty her bedpan?

SKIP. Ah don't like to do that.

LU ANN. Ah know, ah know. But it's got to be done.

SKIP. Ah don't like it, Lu Ann, ah really don't. It makes me throw up.

LU ANN. Well, ah'll do it later.

SKIP. Mah stomach jest turns over and over and . . .

LU ANN. Ah'll take care of it after supper. What did you do today?

SKIP. Oh, nuthin'. Watched the television for a while.

LU ANN. Anythin' good on?

SKIP. Henry Fonda was on the afternoon Old West Movie.

LU ANN. That's nice. You, uh, you didn't feel sick again, did you?

SKIP. No.

LU ANN. Well, if you feel up to it tomorrow, that front grass shore needs a good mowin'.

SKIP. Ah'll git on it first thing. Ah was thinkin' too that ah could clear out a little patch over by the shed and put us in some tomaters and okrie.

LU ANN. Fine.

SKIP. We could have 'em fresh off the vine, wouldn't that be nice?

LU ANN. Shore would.

SKIP. Shore. Ah'm gonna git right on that. First thing in the mornin'. Uh, Lu Ann, seein' as how ah'm gonna do all that tomorrow, do you think that maybe tonight you could, uh, maybe?

LU ANN. No! No money, Skip.

SKIP. Well, no, no. Ah was jest thinkin', if ah had maybe a dollar or somethin', ah could have me mah supper over to the Dixie Dinette, then you won't have to go through no trouble afixin' me nuthin'.

LU ANN. Now, you know ah keep a tab down there so's you can git you a cheeseburger or a chicken-fried any time you want. All you gotta do is sign for it.

SKIP. Well, ah know, but maybe if ah go over to Rufe Phelps's place to play a little dominoes, then ah could use a little money, don't you reckin?

LU ANN. Now, Skip honey, you know ah cain't give you no spendin' money.

SKIP. (*Whining with childish logic.*) Why not? Why cain't ah? Ah ain't gonna do nuthin' bad. Why cain't ah even have a dollar in mah pocket? A by-God dollar to buy somethin' with, somethin' ah see in the store—a Coke or a Mars bar or somethin'. Play a little dominoes or maybe go to the picture show. Jest some pocket change to rattle, buy some cigarettes outta the machine, git me an ice-cream soda or a magazine there at Billberry's Drugstore. Jest stuff like that, Lu Ann, that's all.

Ah won't buy me no wine, no, sir, not even a beer. They won't let me in Red's place no more. They won't even let me in the door. How can ah git a drink when ah cain't even git in the door? No, ma'am, there jest ain't no way.

LU ANN. You said all this before, Skip. Said you didn't want a drink and couldn't git one. But you did git it, honey, cain't you remember? You got enough to put you in the state hospital in Terrell. You wanna go back up to Terrell?

SKIP. No! No, ah don't wanna go there no more. It was ugly there and them doctors was mean. They put me in a little room and it was cold. They put me in a cage like them chinchillas ah had once. You recollect them chinchillas, Lu Ann, and when it was cold?

LU ANN. Sure, honey. Ah remember, but that's all over now, all gone. We ain't gonna talk about them mean times any more, are we?

SKIP. No, no more mean times.

LU ANN. Wanna watch the television for a while? The Country Jubilee Show'll be on tonight.

SKIP. No. Ah think maybe ah'll go on over to the dinette for mah supper, but ah'm not gonna have no cheeseburger or chicken-fry, ah'm gonna have me an enchilada, then ah'll sign the tab. Sign the tab jest like you said. You know, Lu Ann, it's a funny thing how things boil down, ain't it?

LU ANN. Whattayou mean, Skip?

SKIP. When all that stands between a man and the by-God loony bin is his sister's tab down to the Dixie Dinette.

CHARMAINE. (Entering from the kitchen.) My Gawd, you know, we got them big red piss ants under the sink again?

LU ANN. Ah'll pick up some bug killer tomorrow.

CHARMAINE. Terrific. Maybe Uncle Skip will chug it down with his mornin' bowl of Cream of Wheat.

LU ANN. Charmaine, that's enough of that. Now, if you got school-work to do, why don't you go on up to your room and do it.

CHARMAINE. Can ah take mah radio with me?

LU ANN. Ah don't care. Jest don't play it too loud—you might disturb your grandma.

SKIP. She won't do her homework if she's got that radio.

CHARMAINE. You go to hell!

SKIP. You hear that? Cussin', cussin' at me!

LU ANN. Now that's a by-God 'nuff!

SKIP. She's got that skirt on that you don't like.

CHARMAINE. He's always pickin' on me!

LU ANN. Git on upstairs!

CHARMAINE. Ever'body picks on me! What the hell kinda chance do ah have around here anyway, what with a crazy uncle, a dumb-lookin' daddy, and the goddamned Howdy Wagon for a mama! (*She turns and exits, slamming the door.*)

SKIP. She went over to San Angelo and saw old Dale.

LU ANN. Yeah, I know. Charlie Black's mama told me about it.

SKIP. She said he was fat and dumb-lookin'.

LU ANN. Yeah, well. What'd she expect me to find here in Bradleyville in 1953, the by-God King of England. (*Pause.*) Ah thought you was goin' on down to the dinette.

SKIP. Ah'm goin', ah'm goin'. You know, Lu Ann, ah was thinkin' it might be nice if ah could maybe leave a little tip.

LU ANN. Oh, for Christ's sake!

SKIP. It would be nice now, and you know it. Leave maybe fifty cents there on the counter.

LU ANN. Git on outta here—ah'm tired of lookin' at you.

SKIP. Ah'm goin'.

(*A figure approaches the porch—Skip sees him and stops.*)

LU ANN. Well, what's keepin' you?

SKIP. Somebody's comin'.

LU ANN. Probably one of Charmaine's skinny boyfriends.

SKIP. Nope, it's a grown man.

(*There is a knock at the door.*)

LU ANN. I'll git it. (*She walks to the door.*) What can ah do for you?

BILLY BOB. Mrs. Oberlander?

LU ANN. Yes.

BILLY BOB. Mrs. Lu Ann Hampton Oberlander?

LU ANN. Mrs. Lu Ann Hampton *Laverty* Oberlander, if you want the whole damn handle. Who are you?

BILLY BOB. Ah'm Billy Bob, Billy Bob Wortman.

LU ANN. Billy Bob! Well, Jesus Christ on a crutch. Come on in this house and let me look at you. (*She opens the door and lets Billy Bob in. He wears a black suit and horn-rimmed glasses. His hair is stylishly mod and he now sports a small mustache.*) Lookee here, Skip, it's old Billy Bob—the old preacher boy himself.

SKIP (*Shaking hands.*) Howdy, Billy Bob.

BILLY BOB. Hello, Skip, how are you?

SKIP. Fine, fine.

LU ANN. Well, sit down, Billy Bob, or do we call you Reverend nowadays?

BILLY BOB. No, no, just Billy Bob. Plain old Billy Bob. (*He notices Lu Ann's bare feet—she sees this and scurries back to her chair to put her shoes on.*)

LU ANN. Well, sit down, plain old Billy Bob. Make yourself at home. God, it's good to see you.

BILLY BOB. Well, it's marvelous to see you, Lu Ann.

LU ANN. *Marvelous?* Listen to that, Skip, listen to mah little old high-school boyfriend usin' them big words.

SKIP. Sounds pretty good.

LU ANN. You wanna cup of coffee or somethin'?

BILLY BOB. No, nothing thanks.

LU ANN. Sit down, Skip. Quit hangin' around back there.

SKIP. Ah better be gittin' on down to the dinette, Lu Ann. (*To Billy Bob.*) Ah'm havin' me an enchilada tonight.

LU ANN. (*Rising and crossing to him.*) Now, Skip, you're comin' right on home now, hear me?

SKIP. Yeah, ah'll be right on back in.

LU ANN. Well, don't . . . you know.

SKIP. Ah know, ah know. See you all later. (*He exits.*)

LU ANN. (*Looking out of door.*) God, ah hope he don't . . .

BILLY BOB. I know about Brother Hampton's illness, Lu Ann.

LU ANN. Yeah, well, it's nuthin' to trouble yourself about there, Billy Bob.

BILLY BOB. It's my job to trouble myself, Lu Ann.

LU ANN. What? Oh, hell, ah plumb forgot about you bein' a preacher, Billy Bob. My goodness, imagine that. Well, let me look at you. By gollies, that little old mustache is a dandy, ain't it?

BILLY BOB. Yes, well, my congregation rather likes it: it gives me some dignity, don't you think?

LU ANN. Oh, shore. It shore does.

BILLY BOB. I didn't think you'd recognize me with it on.

LU ANN. Oh pshaw, Billy Bob, ah'd know your old hide if ah saw it hangin' on a fence post. Sit down.

BILLY BOB. Yes, thank you.

LU ANN. You know, Billy Bob, ah was real proud to hear you had graduated over there at the Texas Christian University. Ah was livin' in Snyder at the time and my mama wrote me all about it, even sent me the clippings from the *Bradleyville Record.*

BILLY BOB. Well, that's nice.

LU ANN. Oh, shore. Ah even read about you gittin' married. You married a Fort Worth girl, didn't you?

BILLY BOB. Yes, I met Maxine in school. She's a fine woman.

LU ANN. Well, ah jest bet she is. Now, let's see, you have three or is it four children, Billy Bob?

BILLY BOB. Four. Four fine boys.

LU ANN. Well, ain't that nice.

BILLY BOB. You just have the one girl, don't you?

LU ANN. Yes, little Charmaine. Well now, listen to me say *little* Charmaine. She's nearly a growed-up woman now.

BILLY BOB. How old is she?

LU ANN. Seventeen. Can you imagine?

BILLY BOB. My, my.

LU ANN. Yes, she's a chore sometimes, but mostly she's a blessin'. Ah've really got a kick outta watchin' her grow up. Spoiled the devil out of her. But, shoot, what are kids for if it ain't to spoil a little bit?

BILLY BOB. Yes, my boys can be quite the little rascals sometimes too.

LU ANN. Ah wish sometimes that Corky and me coulda give her a little brother or sister—but, well, it jest weren't meant to be.

BILLY BOB. Yes, my mother wrote me about the accident—a real tragedy.

LU ANN. Yes, it was, we wasn't married but a couple of years when it happened. He was out on the job, you see, when his pickup was hit by one of them road machines.

BILLY BOB. Was he killed instantly?

LU ANN. No, he lived for about six or eight hours. 'Course he was busted up so bad there weren't much hope. They got him over to the county hospital and he passed away there. Ah got to see him once affore he died.

BILLY BOB. That was a blessing.

LU ANN. Yes, it was. They had him in a room with these curtains all around. Poor old Corky, he was all bandaged up with tubes and bottles all over him. When ah got there he opened his eyes and moved his hand a little bit and sorter motioned to me, so ah bent down close to his head and he whispered to me real low like, "Lu Ann, Lu Ann, it hit me again, a buffalo, the biggest goddamn buffalo ah ever seed."

BILLY BOB. What did he mean?

LU ANN. Oh, it was just sort of an old joke we had.

BILLY BOB. You ever think of marrying again?

LU ANN. Oh, Lordy, no. Right after Corky was killed Mama had her stroke and ah jest sorter settled in to look after her. Ah had already quit my job at the beauty shop so ah got me this-here job drivin' the Howdy Wagon over to Big Spring.

BILLY BOB. You like the work?

LU ANN. Shore. 'Course ah gotta drive over there of a mornin', but it's not far. And then I like meetin' new people. We git names of new folks movin' into town, you see, and then we drive the Howdy Wagon over to their house and hand out these-here free coupons.

BILLY BOB. What are they good for?

LU ANN. Why, all sorts of thangs. Free bucket of Colonel Sanders' Kentucky Fried Chicken, two free bundles of wash at the Washateria, free round of miniature golf, five gallons of Fina gasoline, six-pack of Coors beer . . . oops, shouldn't of said that, ah reckin.

BILLY BOB. That's okay.

LU ANN. Well, anyway, all sorts of things like that. It's to help the new folks git on to the town, you see.

BILLY BOB. Yes, I understand.

LU ANN. Where do you live now, Billy Bob?

BILLY BOB. Kansas City.

LU ANN. Well, think of that. How do you like the big-city life?

BILLY BOB. We like it very much. I have a fine church there, fine congregation.

LU ANN. Well, ah jest bet you do.

BILLY BOB. Yes, it's nice to be settled down for a while. I'm afraid I've put my family through quite some strain moving around all these years. You knew that I was in missionary work, didn't you?

LU ANN. Ah heard somethin' about it.

BILLY BOB. Oh, yes, indeed. We're here for a little visit. So when I heard you were in town, why, I just had to look you and your mother up. You're about the last of the old high-school gang that's still left around.

LU ANN. Yeah, nobody stays in the little towns any more.

CHARMAINE. (Offstage.) Mama, I cain't work these goddamn algebra problems!

LU ANN. Well, figger it out for yourself. I got company down here.

CHARMAINE. Who?

LU ANN. Billy Bob Wortman.

CHARMAINE. Who the hell's that?

LU ANN. An old friend of mine from high school.

CHARMAINE. Big deal! (Sound of a door slamming.)

LU ANN. Confounded kids. Come out on the porch, Billy Bob, ah believe it's a little cooler.

BILLY BOB. Fine. (They stand for a moment looking out.) Bradleyville. Do they still put the Christmas lights on the water tower every year?

LU ANN. Shore.

BILLY BOB. I guess nothing much has changed in town, has it?

LU ANN. Oh, we have a few new things.

BILLY BOB. Sure enough?

LU ANN. Uh-huh. The Dairy Queen put in a new parking lot and the drive-in's got two screens now.

BILLY BOB. Boy, old Pete Honeycutt would have loved that.

LU ANN. Yeah, ah reckon. Let's see now, the bank's got a whole new front on it, and then of course there's always Mumford County Estates.

BILLY BOB. What's that?

LU ANN. Oh, that's a lake-development outfit we got out to Lake Bradleyville.

BILLY BOB. Really?

LU ANN. Shore. Floyd Kinkaid and Clarence Sickenger got 'em a whole bunch of homes and boathouses and such like out there.

BILLY BOB. Well, that's progress, I guess.

LU ANN. Shore is. They were gonna put 'em in a golf course but they couldn't get the grass to grow!

BILLY BOB. You know, it's funny, Lu Ann, but I never figured you would stay here in Bradleyville.

LU ANN. Ah did leave once. Got as far as Snyder. Aw, I don't know, Billy Bob, ah spoze ah never did think much further than this-here town —never hankered to. You recollect that time when you and me was spozed to go on the senior picnic and ah run out on you and went to San Angelo with old Dale Laverty?

BILLY BOB. I'll never forget it—my heart was broken for a whole week.

LU ANN. Well, ah think maybe it was then that mah life jest sorter dug itself in. Kindly found its little hollow to stay in. You went on to the college and all them other places, but I jest started a-standin' still. Ah run out on a picnic and ran straight into a rut, you might say—even old Corky couldn't pull me outta it, bless his soul.

BILLY BOB. Oh, I don't know, Lu Ann, there isn't really a lot more in the big cities that isn't right here in Bradleyville.

LU ANN. How's come you never played any basketball while you was there at T.C.U.?

BILLY BOB. My word, you had to be good to play ball there. I was just a little old Bradleyville boy, just wasn't up to snuff.

LU ANN. But you was good, Billy Bob, you was real good.

BILLY BOB. Oh, not really.

LU ANN. But ah recollect you playin' over to Snyder that time—mah, how I used to cheer for you. You recall that, Billy Bob, and the time you-all dyed your hair green?

BILLY BOB. Well, that was a long time ago.

LU ANN. You know, mah mama once told me that them times would be the happiest of mah life, and lookin' back on it all, ah believe she mighta been right. Lordy, but it was fun, wasn't it, Billy Bob? The pep rallies, the bonfires, all them dances . . .

BILLY BOB. Paintin' up them posters when Pete Honeycutt ran for president of the senior class.

LU ANN. Mary Beth Johnson, Eveline Blair, and me leadin' the cheers. Goin' over to the Billberry's Drugstore after the home games with Pete and Ruthie Lee Lawell . . .

BILLY BOB. For chocolate Cokes.

LU ANN. That's right! Pickin' on poor old Milo Crawford. Remember all that, Billy Bob? You know, sometimes when ah'm here alone, ah get out my old Bradleyville High yearbook and just go through it lookin' at them pictures and rememberin'. You ever do that?

BILLY BOB. It's a waste of the Lord's time to dwell on the past, Lu Ann.

LU ANN. Oh, pshaw. The Lord's got lots of time to waste. It's us the clock runs down on! You know, Billy Bob, it's a funny thing, but ah'm about the same age mah mama was when you and me was in high school. My God, ain't that somethin'? It's like ah was her and Charmaine was me and ever'body around us got old and different lookin'.

BILLY BOB. Am I so old and different lookin'?

LU ANN. Oh, no, no, of course not. That's one thing about dwellin' in the past. People you loved back then stay the same. You're still old sweet-smilin', goof-off, green-headed Billy Bob Wortman. That preacher suit and mustache don't fool me none.

BILLY BOB. Yes, well. I haven't really got a lot of time left, Lu Ann. Do you think I could see your mother now?

LU ANN. Why shore. My gosh, here ah am runnin' off at the mouth as usual. Ah'll bring her right on out. We keep her in the downstairs bedroom now because of the wheelchair. (*She goes to the Up-Center door.*) She don't recognize people much any more, so don't feel bad now if she don't know you.

BILLY BOB. Yes, of course, I understand.

(Lu Ann *exits. Billy Bob looks at his watch and fidgets about the room. He glances through Charmaine's magazine and drops it distastefully. Lu Ann re-enters with Claudine in the wheelchair. Her hair is totally white, her waxen hands lie limply on her lap. The stroke has paralyzed one side of her face and uncontrollable saliva drools from her mouth, which Lu Ann wipes away from time to time with a clean handkerchief.*)

LU ANN. Here we are. You got a visitor, Mama. Billy Bob Wortman's come all the way from Kansas City for a little visit, ain't that nice? You remember Billy Bob Wortman, don't you, Mama?

BILLY BOB. How are you, Mrs. Hampton?

LU ANN. Why, she's jest as fine as she can be, aren't you, Mama? Be up and outta this old wheelchair just any old day now. Don't you know Billy Bob, Mama? Mah old boyfriend from high school, he's come a long way to see you and say howdy.

(Claudine *gives no sign of recognition at all, simply stares straight ahead.*)

BILLY BOB. (*Taking Claudine's hand.*) Hello there, Mrs. Hampton, how are you? (*Nothing— He drops her hand.*) Can she speak at all, Lu Ann?

LU ANN. No, not a word since her stroke. Ah think that's the biggest shame of the whole business, her not bein' able to talk, 'cause that's one thing Mama loved to do. Couldn't sew, hated to cook, and never read nuthin' but the funny papers, but, oh my, how she loved to talk.

BILLY BOB. Will she be like this from now on—I mean, what do the doctors say?

LU ANN. They say she ain't never goin' to come outta this, not on this earth anyway. So ah jest keep her clean an' fed and ah look after her the best way ah kin.

BILLY BOB. You know, Lu Ann, there are homes for people in her condition. I could look into the church home in Sweetwater if you like.

LU ANN. This is her home, Billy Bob.

BILLY BOB. Well, yes, I know, but it must be a terrible burden.

LU ANN. Aw, it ain't so bad, at least thisaway the burden is mostly on my body—if ah sent her off somewhere, the burden would be on my heart. You know, Billy Bob, them doctors told me that Mama would be a vegetable for the rest of her life—can you imagine that? A vegetable! Hell, my mama ain't no vegetable, she's a flower, a great old big pretty flower.

BILLY BOB. Yes, a creature of God.

LU ANN. You bet.

BILLY BOB. Well, Lu Ann, I really must be going now.

LU ANN. Yep, ah speck them boys will be a-missin' their daddy.

BILLY BOB. It was fine to see you again, Lu Ann.

LU ANN. Well, it was all mah pleasure, Billy Bob. Don't be such a stranger any more, you come on back any time and bring the missus and them boys, you hear?

BILLY BOB. Yes, I'll do that. Well, goodbye, Lu Ann, and may the Lord stay by your side.

LU ANN. So long, Billy Bob, and may, uh . . . may you have lots of luck. (Billy Bob *exits. Lu Ann stands for a moment watching out the screen door, then she turns and comes back into the room.*) Well now, weren't that somethin', Mama? Who would have guessed that one day old Billy Bob would have him a church way up in Kansas City. Jest cain't ever tell, can you, Mama? Jest cain't ever tell. Oh, hell, look at the time, we done missed most of the Country Jubilee. (*She crosses to the television.*) You know, Mama, if ah'd have played mah cards right ah probably could have been Mrs. Billy Bob Wortman today. That's right, missionary's wife way up there in Kansas City, helpin' to spread the Word. (*She giggles.*) But, you know, Mama, ah jest never could cotton to that boy's name. Billy Bob Wortman. Why, it's jest plain silly-soundin'. (*She flicks on the set.*) (*The lights dim as the twang of country music floods into the room.*)

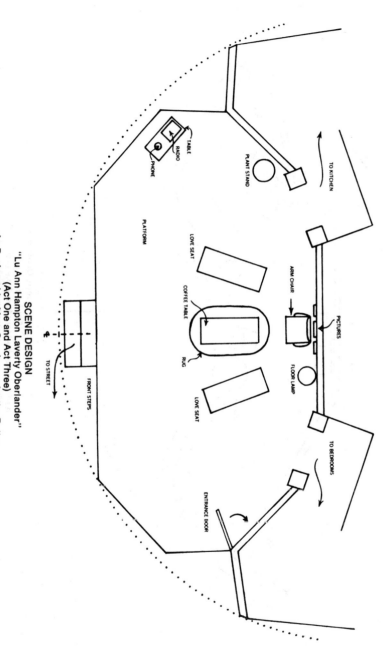

SCENE DESIGN
"Lu Ann Hampton Laverty Oberlander"
(Act One and Act Three)
As Designed by Mary Sue Jones, for the Dallas
Theater Center Production (Thrust Stage)

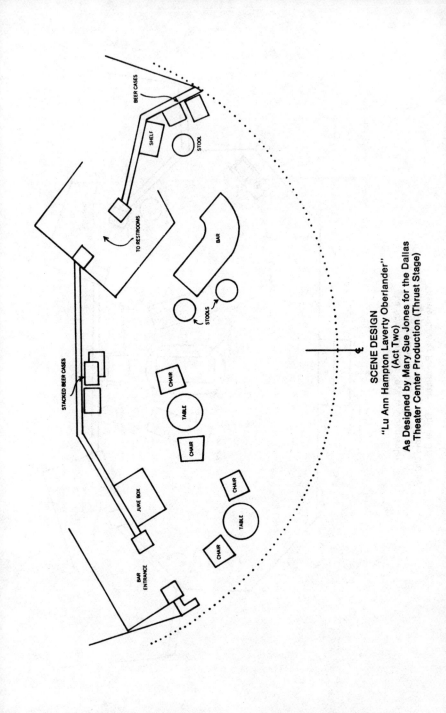

SCENE DESIGN
"Lu Ann Hampton Laverty Oberlander"
(Act Two)
As Designed by Mary Sue Jones for the Dallas
Theater Center Production (Thrust Stage)

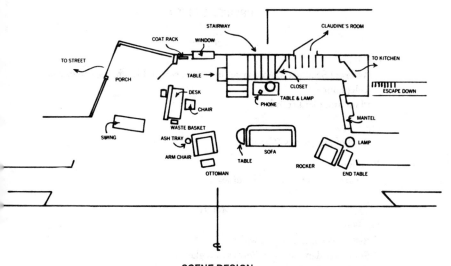

SCENE DESIGN
"Lu Ann Hampton Laverty Oberlander"
(Act One and Act Three)
As Designed by Ben Edwards, for the Washington, D.C.
and New York Productions (Proscenium Stage — with Optional Stairway)

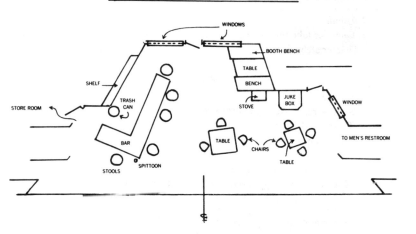

SCENE DESIGN
"Lu Ann Hampton Laverty Oberlander"
(Act Two)
As Designed by Ben Edwards, for the Washington, D.C.
and New York Productions (Proscenium Stage)

PROPERTY LIST

Act One

On Stage
Assorted Sears-catalogue-type furniture: sofa, table, chairs, radio, etc.
Telephone
Plant and plant stand

Off Stage
Bowl of tangerines (Claudine)

Personal
Cigarettes & matches (Claudine)

Act Two

On Stage
Beer advertisements, on walls
Small wooden bar, with bottles and glasses
Tables & chairs
Juke-box
Sign: WE RESERVE THE RIGHT TO REFUSE SERVICE TO
ANYONE
Checkers set
Potato chips, on display rack

Personal
Dime for juke-box (Corky)
Small notebook (Milo)

Act Three

On Stage
Slipcovers, on Act One furniture
TV set
Magazine (Charmaine)
Transistor radio
Color portrait of Charmaine
New lamp, new rug, different plant in plant stand

Off Stage
Two bags of groceries (Lu Ann)
Wheelchair

Personal
Handkerchief (Lu Ann)